EPIC DOG TRICKS

KAYLIN HAUGEN

EPIC DOG TRICKS

60 IMPRESSIVE STUNTS TO ENGAGE AND CHALLENGE YOUR PET

PAGE STREET PUBLISHING CO.

PAGE STREET
PUBLISHING CO.

First published in 2026 by

Page Street Publishing Co.

27 Congress Street, Suite 1511

Salem, MA 01970

www.pagestreetpublishing.com

Distributed by Macmillan, sales in Canada by The Canadian Manda Group.

30 29 28 27 26 1 2 3 4 5

ISBN-13: 979-8-89003-458-8

Library of Congress Control Number: 2025948490

Edited by Marissa Giambelluca

Cover and book design by Elena Van Horn for Page Street Publishing Co.

Photography by Holly Hildreth

Printed and bound in China

For the millions of dogs in shelters and rescues around the world who are waiting for someone to see their potential

CONTENTS

THE MODEL DOG 67

THE HELPER DOG 93

THE HOBBY DOG 119

THE CIRCUS DOG 147

My dog Luna inspired my passion for trick training.

INTRODUCTION

They say, "You can't teach an old dog new tricks," but that couldn't be further from the truth. There isn't a dog out there who can't learn something new when you approach training with a positive mindset and a willingness to meet your dog where they're at. Whether your dog is a bright-eyed puppy or a frosted-faced senior, a purebred show dog or a Heinz® 57 rescue, a confident go-getter or a timid wallflower, one thing is certain: They are capable of learning incredible tricks!

WHERE IT ALL BEGAN

My passion for giving every dog a chance grew from my experience adopting our first family dog when I was eight years old. We went to the local shelter to meet a yellow Labrador we'd seen online, but when we learned he'd already been adopted, a shelter volunteer introduced us to a speckled blue mixed breed. Pepper and I were inseparable for the next decade, and we spent countless hours going for walks and "training" together. Really, I knew nothing about dog training, but Pepper and I had a special connection that I'll always treasure.

Fast-forward to adulthood, when my husband Caleb and I were eager to adopt a dog of our own. We applied with several rescues and stumbled across the profile of a little white dog with red ears, named Lavern. I thought, "I don't want a small dog," and moved on. Shortly after, Lavern's foster actually contacted us and suggested that we meet her, and I'm forever thankful that we did. We fell in love instantly and brought home Luna (the new name her fosters had given her) that weekend.

Luna settled into our lives seamlessly, and I couldn't wait to start teaching her tricks. At first, our progress was extremely slow; Luna didn't seem motivated, and she just wasn't getting it. I remember thinking, "I guess tricks aren't her thing." Little did I know where we'd end up! As we continued working together, I learned so much about how to adapt my training to what she needed and watched her confidence blossom. Five years later, Luna knows upward of 200 tricks and has a zest for demonstrating her skills and learning new things!

I found so much joy in bonding with Luna through trick training that I decided to share our experience in hopes of inspiring others to do the same with their dogs. In the fall of 2020, I began sharing trick tutorials and snapshots of our training on Instagram, and since then have been blown away by the community we've built and the opportunities we've had, from being featured on the *Rachael Ray Show* to writing this book! Most importantly, I have been encouraged daily by stories of people enjoying learning alongside their dogs, which was my goal all along.

A few years later, I had the opportunity to begin teaching trick classes at a local dog-training club, and I have experienced firsthand how every dog is capable of learning tricks. Dogs big and small, young and old, overzealous and apprehensive, have all been able to achieve "aha!" moments, and there is no better feeling than watching teams celebrate those wins. I want YOU to experience that same joy!

WHY SHOULD YOU TEACH YOUR DOG TRICKS?

Trick training is more than just an entertaining pastime; it's a great avenue to build your dog's confidence, strengthen your bond, improve communication, and provide mental enrichment and physical exercise. Dog tricks are incredibly adaptable for every dog and situation, and anyone can experience these benefits in the comfort of their own living room!

CONFIDENCE

Trick training gives your dog the opportunity to make choices and be the one in control. When they're rewarded for problem solving and offering behaviors, it helps them become more willing to try new things. Many tricks also allow your dog to interact with novel props that move and make noise, which can help them learn that new, weird things aren't scary.

BONDING

Teaming up with your dog to learn a new trick is a low-stakes and highly rewarding way to spend time together. As you celebrate the wins together, your dog learns that engaging in training is fun, and it adds so much joy to the time you spend together.

COMMUNICATION

Trick training provides a great context to practice communicating clearly with your dog. You have to find the best way to show your dog what you want them to do and to tell them that they've done it correctly. In return, your dog also learns how better to read your cues.

Trick training is a great way to bond with your dog!

ENRICHMENT

When learning new tricks and practicing old ones, your dog has to use their brain! Trick training requires your dog to concentrate and problem solve, which can put their natural curiosity to good use. When coupled with other enrichment activities, trick training is an excellent way to help reduce boredom and mentally satisfy your dog.

EXERCISE

Tricks can be a useful outlet for physical energy, whether they're active stunts or low-energy skills that still involve movement. When practiced carefully, tricks work your dog's muscles and help them develop better body awareness.

USING THIS BOOK

Whether your dog is brand new to learning tricks or already a seasoned performer, this book has something for you. Trick training doesn't have to be complicated, so I've laid out 60 of my favorite tricks in just five key steps or less. The steps for each trick will give you an easy-to-follow framework that breaks the training process down into small, attainable goals. My aim with this simple structure is to set up you and your dog to confidently proceed through the training process without moving too fast or getting stuck questioning what you should do next. As you work through these lessons, you'll be amazed at how incredible tricks can come together in just a few simple steps!

The tricks in this book are organized by theme, with tricks at a variety of difficulty levels throughout. These tricks do not need to be taught in the order that they are presented; you can explore skills in any order you choose. That said, some tricks include "foundations," which are skills that your dog must learn prior to learning a particular trick. In those cases, be sure to master the prerequisites first, to help set your dog up for success!

To get started, pick a trick that plays to your dog's strengths, try a trick that makes you smile, or opt for a challenge; wherever you begin, you and your dog are sure to have a blast along the way!

BRAIN BREAKS

Between sections of tricks, you will encounter "Brain Breaks," which are simple enrichment activities to try with your dog outside of trick training. The term "enrichment" encompasses experiences that improve your dog's well-being by allowing them to use their instincts and abilities. Trick training is one great opportunity for enrichment; it challenges your dog to problem solve and engages their body. However, just as people benefit from participating in a variety of hobbies, dogs need a variety of enrichment opportunities to help them live a content and fulfilled life. "Brain Breaks" are great ways to get your dog in the zone for a training session or wind down when you've finished training. By spending time training your dog and engaging in activities like these, you're well on your way to giving your dog the best life ever!

Kaylin Haugen

For some dogs, play is the perfect reward!

TRICK TRAINING 101

Before you begin teaching your dog incredible new tricks, it's time for you to attend trick school! Let's dive into the foundational concepts, lingo, and best practices that will equip you to train your dog effectively.

SETTING UP FOR SUCCESS

Creating the ideal training conditions for your dog is just as important as anything you do during training. Before you start working, meet your dog's needs: Allow them to go potty, exercise them through a walk or play, and make sure they aren't too hungry or too stuffed.

Start in a low-distraction environment, such as a room in your home where there aren't other pets or people who could distract your dog. You can move to more lively environments later, but a crowded park is typically not the best starting point.

Train on a padded surface with good traction, such as a carpet or rubber floor mats. This is especially important when practicing tricks that involve jumping or large movements, to protect your dog's joints and to prevent slipping and falling.

Begin training sessions by reviewing skills your dog knows well and enjoys performing, to get your dog engaged and feeling confident. Then, transition to working on new tricks.

Keep training sessions short, around 5 to 15 minutes. If you want to train more, you can do several sessions throughout the day. Stretching these training sessions too long can lead to fatigue and frustration, so strive to end your training sessions while your dog is still having fun!

POSITIVE REINFORCEMENT

Tricks should be taught exclusively using positive reinforcement, which focuses on rewarding your dog for a behavior so that they are more likely to do it again. In the context of trick training, this typically involves giving your dog a treat or toy after they perform a trick.

FOOD REWARDS

Treats are the most common type of reinforcement. To avoid overfeeding and upset tummies, use pea-sized rewards that are high quality and low calorie, and limit treats to no more than 10 percent of your dog's daily intake. Test out different treats to find what your dog likes best. A few of my go-to treats include:

- Freeze-dried meat
- Novel dry dog foods
- Plain chicken
- Low-fat cheese sticks
- Turkey hot dogs

Consider saving high-value treats, such as real meat, for more difficult tasks. Try mixing a few types of treats together in your treat pouch to make a "trail mix" of unpredictable rewards!

TOYS

For some dogs, a quick game of tug or fetch is even more effective than rewarding with treats. This works well for dogs who already have a strong toy drive, and it's beneficial if your dog has a reliable "drop it" cue so that you can transition back to training. Although I use the term "treats" to refer to rewards throughout this book, you can substitute toys in most situations. It's all about what your dog finds most rewarding!

MARKERS

Your dog needs to understand the exact behavior you are rewarding, so they can repeat it. The best way to communicate this is by using a marker, a distinct signal that identifies the moment your dog performs a desired behavior and which is followed by a reward. Imagine your marker as a camera shutter; if you take the photo too early or too late, you aren't capturing the right picture, so you have to be precise!

You can use a clicker to mark when your dog does the correct behavior.

Common markers include:

- Short words, such as "yes," "good," or "nice"
- A clicker (a handheld device with a button that makes a unique sound)
- For deaf dogs: visual signs, such as a thumbs-up
- For deafblind dogs: a gentle tap on the dog's head, chest, or other body part that they feel comfortable with

A marker is only meaningful if you teach your dog that it means a reward is coming. Before using your marker during training, pair it with a reward by marking, then giving a treat, repeating until your dog associates it with an incoming reward. During these pairing sessions, your dog doesn't have to do anything; you are just teaching them that marker = treat!

Some people use different markers to communicate where the reward will be delivered, treats vs toys, and completed vs ongoing behaviors. Throughout this book, you will see the phrase "mark and reward" to refer to using whichever type(s) of markers you choose, then giving a reward.

JACKPOT!

When your dog makes exceptional progress toward learning a trick, give them an extra exciting reward, called a "jackpot." This can be multiple treats in row and/or a special kind of treat or toy reserved only for jackpots. Jackpots are a great way to increase your dog's motivation to perform that same behavior again.

WHAT IF MY DOG DOES THE WRONG THING?

When training with positive reinforcement, punishing your dog for doing the wrong behavior (including saying "no," "uh-oh," or "oops") is off-limits. Punishment doesn't tell your dog what they *are* supposed to do, and it has a negative impact on engagement, motivation, and trust. Instead, if your dog offers the wrong behavior, ask yourself these questions:

- Have my dog's needs been met?
- Is the environment too distracting or stressful?
- Have we been training for too long?
- Could my dog be in pain or uncomfortable?
- Has my dog mastered the foundations needed for this behavior?
- Am I moving too quickly or expecting too much of my dog?
- Am I communicating clearly with my dog?
- How can I change my approach or expectations to make my dog more successful?

Address the issues that apply (which sometimes means simply taking a break!) and try again. Providing your dog with more support, going back to an easier step, or altering your approach is often all that's needed to help your dog succeed.

HOW TO TEACH A TRICK

There are three primary techniques used to teach a trick: luring, capturing, and shaping.

LURING

Luring involves holding a treat at your dog's nose and steering them to perform the desired behavior. For dogs who are new to luring, start by teaching them to follow a lure. Hold a treat at their nose and guide them to walk around, rewarding for following the lure without excessively nibbling or licking your hand.

Luring is a common method for teaching tricks.

To fade out a food lure and make a trick more independent, transition to luring with an empty hand once your dog can reliably perform the behavior with food. Gradually lure more subtly until your luring motion morphs into just a hand signal.

CAPTURING

Capturing is a way to teach your dog to perform natural behaviors on cue. To capture a trick, wait for your dog to do the behavior on their own (e.g., wait for them to lie down), marking and rewarding when they do so. Over time, they will likely offer this behavior more, giving you more chances to reinforce it. Add a cue by saying the word (or doing a hand signal) just as your dog begins to do it. After many repetitions, give your cue and jackpot if your dog performs the skill in response!

SHAPING

Shaping is a dog-directed training technique involving rewarding small approximations toward the end-goal. For example, to teach your dog to get into a box, you could let them investigate on their own and mark and reward these progressions:

Looking at box ➔ Moving toward box ➔
Putting 1 or 2 paws in box ➔
Putting all paws in box

The two keys to shaping are: (1) progress in tiny steps, and (2) mark and reward with precise timing. Shaping is an excellent strategy that allows hesitant dogs to move at their own pace and develop confidence.

CUES

A cue is a signal that prompts your dog to perform a learned behavior. The main types of cues referenced in this book are hand signals and verbal cues. Touch cues (e.g., tapping your dog on the shoulder to cue "spin") are a common alternative for deafblind dogs. In most cases, you can use any type of cue for a trick.

VISUAL CUES AND HAND SIGNALS

Visual cues, most often hand signals, use body language to ask your dog to do something, such as lowering your palm toward the floor to cue "down." Hand signals can evolve from the way you lure a dog to learn a new trick, but you can also pair a trick with a hand signal when not using luring.

VERBAL CUES

Verbal cues include words, phrases, and other sounds. Wait to introduce a verbal cue until your dog understands the behavior. Saying, "Roll over! Roll over!" before your dog knows how to do that, doesn't help them develop a meaningful connection. Once your dog can execute a trick, add a verbal cue by saying it *before* your dog does the trick. If your dog has already learned a hand signal, the progression looks like this:

Say verbal cue ➔ Give hand signal ➔
Dog does trick ➔ Reward

Eventually, you can cue using just your verbal once your dog learns the new association.

CUE TRANSFERS

A cue transfer is a method to teach your dog a new cue for a trick they already know. Pairing a trick with a verbal cue when your dog already knows a hand signal is a type of cue transfer. Cue transfers are a great way to create entertaining cues for tricks. The sequence looks like this:

Give new cue → Give old cue →
Dog does trick → Reward

After many repetitions, you can fade out the old cue. Tricks like "Take a Selfie" (page 89), "Fetch a Tissue" (page 102), and "Read Cue Cards" (page 143) demonstrate cue transfers in action.

FREQUENTLY ASKED QUESTIONS

How long should I spend on each step of a trick?

More often than not, you won't move through every step of a trick in a single training session. Continue working on a given step until your dog can execute it with at least 90 percent accuracy; sometimes, this means spending multiple training sessions on a single step! When resuming working on a trick in a new training session, review previous steps before moving on to the next.

How long does it take to master a trick?

In short—it depends! Some dogs may be able to master a particular trick in a day, while others may work on a certain trick for weeks. Going slow and steady is important. Rather than rushing a trick, progress in small approximations for the best results.

How do I know my dog has mastered a trick?

In general, your dog has mastered a trick once they can consistently perform it on cue, without luring or heavy prompting. A further level of fluency involves proofing and generalizing a trick, meaning that your dog can perform it in different contexts. For tricks like "Hold" (page 37) and "Fetch" (page 41), generalization extends to being able to perform the trick with various objects.

What supplies do I need for trick training?

The most basic supplies needed for any training session include a treat pouch and rewards. Beyond that, most of the materials noted in this book are household objects or props you can find at a thrift store. You will see these two items referred to often:

- **Platform**—An elevated surface that your dog can fit their entire body on. This can be a commercial dog-training platform, rigid couch cushions or a firm dog bed, or a large piece of wood with a yoga mat or traction tape on top.
- **Foot target**—A smaller elevated surface that your dog can comfortably fit two paws on. Rubber feed bowls, firm foam mats, and pieces of wood with a yoga mat or traction tape on top work well.

THE FOUNDATIONS

Before your dog can learn incredible tricks, they need to master the foundations. These basic tricks and skills serve as the starting point for many of the tricks in this book (and countless others!). By taking the time to teach your dog the tricks in this section and practicing them until they are fluent, you will set your pup up to be able to master advanced tricks with ease. Although your dog does not have to know all of these building blocks to start their trick-training journey, you'll find that these key skills unlock a world of possibilities!

SIT

"Sit" is a quintessential dog trick and is the first skill that many teach their dogs. Since it is a natural behavior, many dogs learn to sit on cue quickly. When teaching "Sit," be careful not to overuse it; there is no need for your dog to always sit before receiving a treat. "Sit" is simply one of many tricks that you can cue your dog to do!

One of the most common methods for teaching your dog to sit is by luring (outlined in the steps that follow), but you can also teach it through capturing: If you simply stand still or take a seat on the couch and wait, your dog is likely to eventually sit down on their own. Mark and reward when they do, and after many repetitions say "sit" just as your dog begins to lower their back end. In time, you can cue "Sit" to ask your dog to do the behavior!

STEPS

1. With your dog standing, hold a treat at their nose and slowly lure up and over their head. As they lift their head to follow the treat, most dogs will naturally rock backward into a sit. Mark as soon as your dog lowers their haunches, rewarding while your dog is still sitting.
2. Lure as in step 1, but without a treat in hand. Gradually lure in a less exaggerated way, to morph your lure into a hand signal. A common signal is to hold your palm facing you and scoop your hand toward your chest, so mimic this motion as you lure.
3. Progress until your dog will sit in response to just a hand signal.
4. Say "sit" before giving your hand signal to add your verbal cue.
5. Proof this skill by asking your dog to sit in a variety of locations and on a variety of surfaces.

Lure up and over your dog's head.

DOWN

Like "Sit" (page 20), "Down" is a common trick that many dog parents teach early on. In the context of trick training, "Down" is the starting point for many fun skills, such as "Roll Over" (page 56) and "Crawl" (page 63).

You can teach it through luring, which is outlined in these steps, or you can capture it when your dog offers it naturally. Set up your dog to be more likely to lie down of their own accord by exercising them first, then settling down in a comfortable location where they are likely to relax. Mark and reward as soon as they lie down, and after many repetitions, begin adding a verbal cue as they start to go into the position. With lots of practice, you can try cueing "Down" with just a word!

FOUNDATIONS

- Sit (page 20)—optional; you could lure your dog to lie down from a standing position

STEPS

1. Starting with your dog in a sit, hold a treat at their nose, and lure diagonally down and forward until they step forward with their front paws. Reward incrementally as your dog progresses closer to lying down; they may just lean forward at first, then step one paw out, and finally walk their front paws forward into a full "Down." Practice until you can lure your dog from a "Sit" to a "Down" in one motion.

Lure your dog to lie down.

2. Lure as in step 1, but without a treat. Fade out the lure, transitioning toward simply motioning downward with a flat palm facing the ground, to create a hand signal.

3. Progress until your dog will lie down in response to just a hand signal.

4. Say "down" before giving your hand signal to add your verbal cue.

5. Practice "Down" in a variety of locations and on a variety of surfaces.

TIP: If your dog is struggling to follow the lure into a "Down" position, try luring them to go under something (e.g., your leg or a chair), to help guide them.

TOUCH

"Touch" is a useful trick in which your dog presses their nose to your hand. You can use a flat palm, closed fist, or two pointed fingers, as your target. Instead of using your hand, you could also teach this skill using a target stick.

A nose touch is a fantastic foundational skill with many practical and trick-training applications. You can cue "Touch" to encourage your dog to actively engage with you or to call them back to you. Nose targeting also provides another way to guide your dog, instead of luring them with a treat, when teaching new tricks. After your dog learns a nose touch, you can teach them tricks that build from it, such as "Tell Me a Secret" (page 86) and "Kiss" (page 85).

STEPS

1. Hold a flat palm upright facing your dog. Most dogs will naturally be curious about your hand and will reach out to sniff it. Mark and reward any movement of their nose toward your hand, even if they don't touch it yet. Use your other hand to place a treat in your outstretched palm, to reward.
2. Gradually progress until your dog purposefully touches their nose to your hand.
3. Add a verbal cue, such as "touch," before holding out your hand.
4. Practice cueing "Touch" with each hand and in different positions, to help proof the skill.

(continued)

Use a target stick for another variation of "Touch."

TOUCH (CONTINUED)

5. To build a sustained nose touch (your dog holds their nose on your hand rather than quickly "pecking" it), try one of these strategies:
   - Continue shaping and jackpot the times your dog holds their touch for a fraction of a second longer, gradually increasing the duration.
   - Move your hand backward while cueing "Touch" to encourage your dog to drive forward; try cueing multiple touches in a row with this strategy.
   - Hold the treat in sight behind your hand to encourage stillness as they lock onto the treat.
   - Consistently reward in your palm, so your dog anticipates where the reward will come from.

TIP: If your dog already knows "Shake" (page 27) and automatically gives you their paw when you hold out your palm, try using a fist for this trick instead.

SHAKE

"Shake" is the most common "fun" trick that people teach their dogs. While it's an adorable trick on its own, teaching your dog to give you their paw also lays the foundation for other tricks that require your dog to use their paws. Tricks like "Wave" (page 68) and "Chorus Line Kicks" (page 157) are essentially extensions of "Shake," and you can use "Shake" to teach your dog to paw other objects in such tricks as "Close a Door" (page 97) and "Turn Off the Lights" (page 112).

An outdated method for teaching this trick involves picking your dog's paw up off the ground, but that method doesn't give them any control of their learning and makes many dogs uncomfortable. We'll explore two better methods for teaching this trick; experiment to see which strategy works best for your pup.

GET IT METHOD

STEPS

1. Hold a treat in a closed fist. Wiggle your hand near your dog's front paws, to entice them to paw at your hand to get the treat. Mark and reward by opening your fist so your dog can get the treat when your dog paws at your hand.
2. Repeat step 1 with an empty, but still closed, hand. Focus on rewarding only when they use the same paw; this will help later to create separate cues for each paw.
3. Hold out an open hand, palm up. Mark and reward when your dog places their paw in your hand.
4. Add a verbal cue, such as "shake" or "paw," before offering your hand.
5. Repeat steps 1–4, using your other hand and waiting for your dog to reach out with their other paw, to teach them to shake with that paw; add a different verbal cue.

(continued)

SHAKE (CONTINUED)

LURING METHOD

STEPS

1. Hold a treat at your dog's nose and slowly lure upward and diagonally so your dog leans toward one side. Mark and reward when your dog lifts their opposite paw off the ground as they reach for the treat.

2. Start a cue transfer by extending your other hand toward your dog's paw (not grabbing it) before doing the luring motion from step 1. Through many repetitions, your dog will begin to anticipate that they should lift their paw after you extend your hand.

3. Position your hand so your dog's paw will naturally land in your palm when they lift their paw. Jackpot when your dog's paw touches your hand.

4. Once your dog begins lifting their paw when your reach out your hand, fade out the upward luring motion by luring without a treat, eventually ceasing luring altogether, and add your verbal cue.

5. Repeat steps 1–4 in the other direction, to teach your dog to give their other paw, adding a different verbal cue.

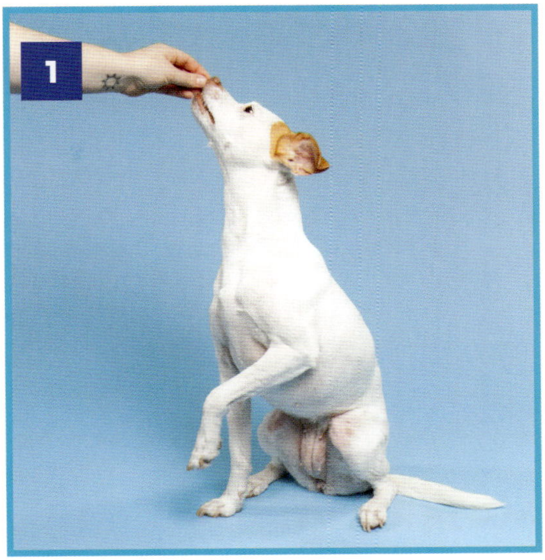

Lure up and to one side until your dog lifts the opposite paw.

FRONT PAWS UP

Before your dog learns entertaining tricks, such as "Pray" (page 59), "Play the Piano" (page 135), and "Pivot" (page 179), they need to learn how to put their front paws up on an object. Teaching "Front Paws Up" not only lays the foundation for specific tricks, but is also a great confidence builder. Teaching your dog to place their paws on a variety of textures and objects that move can help them become more comfortable interacting with new things.

Begin with a wide target, such as a long piece of wood or a commercial dog-training platform. For dogs who are hesitant to step up onto anything, you can even start with a nearly flat target that is easier to step onto. As your dog learns the skill, practice with narrower targets, such as rubber feed bowls; higher targets, such as chairs; and wobbly targets, such as inflatable disks.

MATERIALS

- Platform or foot target

STEPS

1. Position your target between you and your dog. Lure your dog forward and up so that they step onto the target with their front paws. Mark and reward if your dog places even just one paw on the target, progressing until they can step up with both front paws.

2. Lure your dog as in step 1, but without a treat in hand. Fade out the lure, eventually cueing your dog to put their paws on the target by just pointing to the target.

3. Add a verbal cue, such as "paws up," before giving your hand signal.

4. Practice "Front Paws Up" on a variety of targets (couches, steps, and logs are great options!) to proof the skill.

TIP: Some dogs will do better stepping onto a lower target at first; others may pick up the skill faster when being lured onto a higher target (e.g., a chair).

REAR FOOT TARGET

Teaching your dog to place their back paws on a target is a great skill that is helpful for trick training and beyond. This trick helps develop rear-end awareness, which is your dog's ability to know where their back feet are and move them intentionally. Dogs naturally navigate with their front paws while their rear paws follow, so this is a skill dogs need to practice! Rear-end awareness is helpful for such tricks as "Back Up" (page 60) and "Handstand" (page 170), and it also can help your dog balance and navigate more confidently on tricky surfaces.

For this trick, you will teach your dog how to walk forward over a platform and stop with just their back feet on the target. Then, you'll teach your dog how to move backward to place their rear paws up onto the target.

MATERIALS

- Platform

STEPS

1. Position a low platform between you and your dog. Lure your dog to walk forward, up and over the platform, until their front paws step down onto the floor and their rear paws remain on the target. Mark and reward as soon as they reach this position, rewarding several times as they stay there, then reset them behind the platform and repeat.
2. Gradually reduce how much you lure your dog, jackpotting when they stop independently with their rear paws on the target.
3. When your dog is consistently stopping with their back feet on the target, add a verbal cue, such as "feet" or "target," before they walk over the platform.
4. To practice backing up to a rear foot target, cue the behavior as in steps 1–3 and place the reward on the ground just far enough ahead that your dog has to partially step off the platform to retrieve it. If you have spent a lot of time reinforcing your dog for having their back feet on the platform, they are likely to take a step backward to get into that position again. Jackpot! Gradually increase how far ahead you place the treat, so your dog has to step back farther.
5. Fade out the treat placement and just call your dog to you, then use your verbal cue to ask them to back their rear paws onto the platform.

Reward your dog for stepping back to the platform.

GET ON

Teaching your dog to get onto a platform with all four paws, often called "place," is a skill that has many practical applications. In the context of trick training, we will teach this trick as simply cueing your dog to get on an elevated platform, not asking them to automatically go into a specific position like "Down" or stay on the target for an extended period.

Practicing this trick with a variety of novel objects can help boost confidence as your dog learns to interact with new things in an exciting and rewarding context. For trick training, cueing your dog onto a platform can be helpful when you need them to be in a specific place, such as staying behind you when you're teaching "Take a Selfie" (page 89).

MATERIALS

- Platform

STEPS

1. Use a treat to lure your dog to step onto a platform with all four paws. You can reward your dog for just placing one or two paws up at first, then work up to stepping onto the target with all four paws.
2. Once your dog is consistently following the lure and confidently putting all four paws on the platform, repeat the same luring motion from step 1, without a treat in hand. Gradually reduce how much you lure to get your dog to step onto the platform, until your dog will get on when you just motion toward the platform with a hand signal.
3. When your dog is consistently getting onto the platform with a subtle hand gesture, say "place" or "on" before giving your hand signal, to add your verbal cue.
4. Gradually add distance by standing a step farther from the platform, then cueing "Get On." After several successful repetitions, take another step back, continuing to increase the distance until you can send your dog from several feet (about 80 cm) away.
5. Practice on a variety of objects at home and out on walks, to proof this trick!

HOLD

Teaching your dog to hold an object in their mouth on cue unlocks many advanced tricks. Dogs who naturally like to take things in their mouth may catch on to putting this behavior on cue quickly, whereas dogs who are not very mouthy may need you to break down the behavior into small steps.

The item you use initially to teach your dog this trick can make a big difference; a familiar toy can be a good starting point, but you can also use a novel object. Choose something that your dog can easily fit in their mouth, is not too heavy, and is a safe material your dog is comfortable with. You might have to experiment with a few items before finding what works best for your dog.

MATERIALS

- Toy
- Other objects to hold

STEPS

1. Hold your item in front of your dog's mouth. Mark and reward any interaction with the object, such as looking at it, sniffing toward it, or even touching it with their nose.
2. Continue progressing with step 1, jackpotting any time your dog increases their level of interaction with the object. Progress until they momentarily take the object in their mouth while you're holding it. If you're struggling, you can encourage your dog to mouth the object by excitedly moving it around as if playing with a toy.
3. Once your dog will consistently grab the item, begin building duration. Try one of these strategies:
    - Shape duration by marking and rewarding when your dog holds the object for a fraction of a second longer. Always mark while they are still holding the object, and gradually increase the duration.
    - Use a known cue, such as "wait" or "stay," to encourage stillness.
    - Cue "Touch" (page 24) so your dog holds the object longer as they move to your hand.
    - Use "Chin Rest" (page 77) to encourage your dog to stay still with a closed mouth.
    - Use "Tug" (page 38) or "Fetch" (page 41) to playfully increase duration.
4. Add a verbal cue, such as "hold," before giving your dog the object, once they will hold the item for a few seconds.
5. Generalize this skill by practicing with other items. You may have to go back through the steps at first to introduce new items, but over time your dog will catch on to holding new items more quickly.

TUG

While tugging on a toy may seem more like a game than a trick, it's a very useful behavior to put on cue for trick training! Once your dog can pull on a rope or other item when you ask, they'll be ready to learn such tricks as "Open a Door" (page 94) and "Take Off My Shoe" (page 101).

Dogs who already love to play tug with their toys can often learn to transfer this behavior quickly. However, some dogs aren't naturally big fans of tugging, so they may need more time to build this skill from the ground up. For dogs who won't naturally take toys in their mouth, try starting with the steps for "Hold" (page 37), to teach them to grab an object, then shape steps 2 and 3 in this tutorial to build up to pulling. You can reward them with treats rather than play.

MATERIALS

- Toy
- Rope or length of strong fabric (e.g., braided strips of an old shirt or jeans)

STEPS

1. Get out your dog's favorite toy (or a new toy, for even more excitement!) and wiggle, toss, or drag it around to entice them to grab it. Reward your dog for taking the toy in their mouth with their favorite type of play, continuing to make the game fun for your dog.

2. Some dogs will immediately be ready to tug on the toy with you in step 1. For dogs who release the toy quickly, gradually build up to tugging. Try pulling on the toy when it's in their mouth for a fraction of a second, then give them a "win" and release or throw the toy back to them. Repeat, gradually increasing how long your tugging lasts, and always keeping the game fun for your dog.

3. Once your dog will tug on the toy in the context of play, start adding the verbal cue "tug," by saying it as your dog takes the toy in their mouth to tug.

4. Teach your dog to drop the toy on cue. A great way to do this is to present a second, similar toy and reward your dog with it when they drop the first toy. Say "drop it" just before they let go, to add a verbal cue.

5. Generalize your "Tug" cue to other objects. Start with objects similar to toys, such as rope, braids of strong fabric, or even socks. Cue "Tug" and make the item enticing as in steps 1 and 2, rewarding with play (with the new object or another toy) when your dog tugs on it.

FETCH

Just like "Tug" (page 38), "Fetch" may seem more like play than training, but it can be both! Teaching your dog to retrieve objects to your hand paves the way for tricks that involve placing an item in a designated spot, such as "Clean Up Your Toys" (page 106) and "Play Basketball" (page 129). When you are teaching "Fetch," toy-driven dogs may not need food rewards at first. You can introduce food rewards, or reward with an alternative toy to fetch, when you start working on retrieving non-toy objects later.

Dogs who do not naturally fetch toys on their own can still learn how to retrieve as a trick, with some intentional training. For dogs who don't take objects in their mouth, start by teaching "Hold" (page 37), then modify the following steps, building off "Hold" rather than play. Dogs who are less toy-driven will likely learn best when rewarded with treats for holding and eventually retrieving the object.

MATERIALS

- Your dog's favorite toy
- Other items to fetch

STEPS

1. Toss the toy a very short distance away. Praise as soon as your dog grabs the toy, then excitedly encourage them to come back to you with it. Reward when they come back to you with their favorite type of play, such as tugging or tossing the toy again.
2. Hold out your hand when your dog brings back the toy. Wait for them to bring the toy near your hand—even if just momentarily—then immediately reward. Repeat until your dog will consistently bring the toy to your hand.
3. Add a verbal cue, such as "fetch," before you toss the toy.
4. Gradually toss the toy farther away. Also, practice placing the toy, without throwing it, and cueing your dog to go fetch it.
5. Repeat steps 1–4 with other non-toy objects, to start to generalize this skill. You may need to practice "Hold" (page 37) first, to teach your dog to take the new item in their mouth, then work up to retrieving it. The more objects you practice with over time, the quicker your dog will catch on to retrieving new items!

TIP: If your dog isn't bringing the toy near your hand, try cueing "Touch" (page 24), to encourage them to move toward your hand.

BRAIN BREAK

FROZEN FOOD FUN

Frozen food enrichment has rocketed in popularity and is a common activity choice for many dog parents. Filling specially designed dog toys with food and freezing them for your dog to enjoy later is a great way to always have a simple, mentally stimulating activity on hand. Although a lot of people turn to frozen enrichment just to keep their dog occupied for a long time, the benefits go way beyond busywork! Many dogs actually enjoy working for their food, and frozen enrichment is a great way to engage their brain in using foraging and problem-solving skills. Additionally, licking releases endorphins and can have a soothing effect for dogs.

Frozen enrichment toys can be a great addition to your routine when done thoughtfully. Be sure to provide your dog with an appropriate level of challenge. If your find your dog gets frustrated or can't get the food out, try an easier toy (such as a flat lick mat rather than a densely stuffed toy) or skip freezing your filled toys. Always monitor your dog to ensure they aren't chewing up the toy itself. Finally, be mindful not to overfeed your dog. Use a portion of their meal or try some of the low-calorie ideas on this list.

FILLING IDEAS

- Soaked kibble
- Wet dog food
- Bone broth *(homemade or dog-specific brands without added sodium or unsafe seasonings)*
- Goat's milk
- Plain, nonfat yogurt
- Fat-free cottage cheese
- Fresh or blended fruits and veggies
- Applesauce
- Pumpkin puree
- Mashed banana
- Mashed sweet potato
- Baby food *(check that all ingredients are dog-safe)*

THE CLASSIC DOG

When you think about dog tricks, you might envision a dog playfully rolling over or answering the cue "speak" with an enthusiastic bark. Classic tricks like these are widely known and loved for a reason: They're attainable for many dogs to learn, don't require any special props, and have the "aww!" factor! The popular tricks in this chapter are the perfect start to building a repertoire of entertaining tricks, and they provide great opportunities to build your dog's confidence and improve your own training mechanics. Before you know it, you'll both be ready to take your training to the next level!

SPIN

"Spin" is a simple and dynamic skill to learn and is perfect for dogs who are new to trick training. You can teach your dog to turn in a circle by using a simple luring motion that many dogs catch on to quickly. To give this trick an impressive flair, teach your dog to spin in each direction in response to different cues.

Dogs who are shy about things going over their head may be more wary when learning this trick. Try sitting on the ground vs standing up, positioning yourself by your dog's side, or using a target stick to lure your dog instead.

STEPS

1. Use a treat to slowly lure your dog to turn around in a full circle, keeping the treat near their shoulder level. Mark and reward once your dog completes the circle. Repeat, always luring in the same direction.
2. Lure as in step 1, but with an empty hand. Fade the lure into a hand signal by holding your hand with one pointed finger and gradually luring farther away from your dog, progressing until you can cue by flicking your finger in a partial circle.
3. Add a verbal cue, such as "spin," "turn," "twist," or "circle," by saying it before giving your hand signal.
4. After many repetitions, give just your verbal cue and jackpot if your dog spins in response. If they aren't sure what to do, continue to practice step 3.
5. To teach your dog to spin in the other direction, repeat steps 1–4, using your other hand to lure the other way. Be sure to pick a different verbal cue!

TIP: If your dog is hesitant to follow the lure all the way around, try luring just a quarter- or half-circle at first. Toss the treat so they naturally continue the turn as they retrieve it. Slowly work up to a full circle.

SPEAK

Have you ever wished your dog could talk to you? While it's not the same as having a full conversation, teaching them to bark on cue is almost as entertaining. Teaching this trick looks different for every dog, since it's based on what naturally elicits a bark for your dog; it could be seeing their favorite toy, smelling a treat in your hand, or hearing another dog barking!

Dogs who already bark often may have an easier time learning this trick, but even quiet dogs can find their voice. I thought my dog, Luna, would never learn "Speak" because she rarely barks, but I finally discovered something that got her to make some noise—digging! When I cued her to wipe her paws (see page 98), she started huffing and grumbling, and I was able to reward those noises until she truly barked. Now, she is always ready to "speak" up!

STEPS

1. Capture when your dog naturally barks by creating a scenario that makes them likely to bark (e.g., squeaking a toy, fake "barking" at them, or engaging in exciting play). Mark and reward when your dog barks in response.

2. Once your dog is consistently barking in response to your trigger, use a cue transfer to teach them to bark in response to a new cue rather than the trigger. Say a cue, such as "speak," or give a hand signal, such as a "yapping" hand gesture, then give your trigger. Continue marking and rewarding when your dog barks after the trigger. Repeat many times so your dog learns to associate the verbal cue and/or hand signal with the subsequent trigger and barking.

3. Give your verbal cue and/or hand signal and wait before giving your trigger. If your dog barks, give them a huge jackpot! If not, go back to step 2. Intersperse repetitions with your trigger until your dog consistently barks in response to just your new cue.

PLAY DEAD

Hone your dog's acting skills by teaching them the perfect party trick: "Play Dead!" For this entertaining classic, your dog flops onto their side dramatically. Cues like "play dead" or "bang!" are some of the most common names for this trick, but you could also opt for a gentler version by asking your dog to "go to sleep," "take a nap," or even "melt."

When training this trick, you may find that your dog is better at rolling onto one side than the other; test each direction to see which your dog prefers. Train on a soft surface and in a more relaxed environment, to help your dog feel at ease. If you notice your dog is very hesitant to do this trick, it may be uncomfortable for them. Never physically manipulate your dog onto their side, and always prioritize their comfort!

FOUNDATIONS

- Down (page 23)

STEPS

1. Cue "Down;" most dogs will initially lie down in a Sphinx-like position with both hips and rear paws squared up. Slowly lure them to turn their nose toward their shoulder. Mark and reward when they turn just their head, incrementally luring farther until their nose almost reaches their shoulder.

2. Keep luring in this motion until your dog moves from the initial "Sphinx" down to tucking the opposite hip under, jackpotting when they do. Repeat until your dog consistently responds to the lure by rolling onto one hip.

(continued)

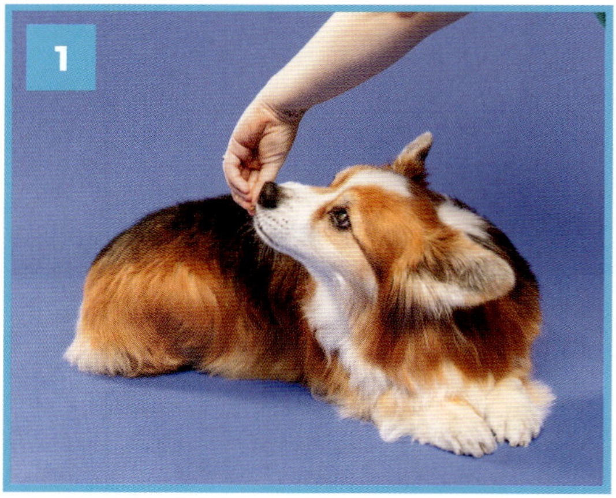

1

Lure your dog's nose to their shoulder.

PLAY DEAD (CONTINUED)

3. Continue the luring arc after your dog tucks their hip under, until they lie flat on their side. Reward multiple times in a row once they are on their side, to reinforce staying still in this position.

4. Fade the lure into a hand signal by practicing the luring motion without a treat. Gradually lure more subtly with your hand in the position you will use for your cue (e.g., a finger gun if you want to call this trick "bang!" or "play dead," or wiggling your fingers for "go to sleep"). Practice until your dog flops onto their side with just a hand signal.

5. Add your verbal cue by saying it before your hand signal.

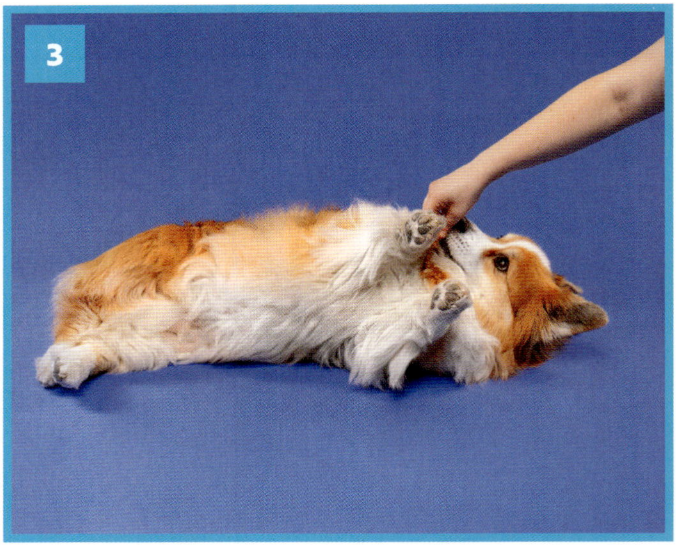

Continue luring until your dog turns onto their side.

BOW

The perfect way to end any trick routine is to take a bow! Many dogs already offer this behavior naturally when they want to play or when they're doing a "big stretch!" One option to teach this trick is to capture it by rewarding when your dog bows on their own and adding a cue to it. We'll look at two other options for teaching this trick from the ground up; for both methods, going slow and breaking the trick into small parts are key for success!

When naming this trick, avoid using the word "bow" as your cue. "Bow" sounds a lot like "down," and given that they are already similar behaviors, your dog could get confused! Words like "ta-da," "curtsy," or even "stretch" are better options.

LURING METHOD

STEPS

1. With your dog standing, imagine a diagonal line running from the tip of their nose to just behind their front paws. Lure down and back along this line. Mark and reward when your dog begins to lean back and dip their shoulders without lying down or stepping back, then quickly "reset" with a second treat in a standing position.
2. Continue to work along this imaginary line until you can lure your dog into a full bow position. As in step 1, reward once in position, then again when your dog stands back up.
3. Build duration holding a bow by rewarding multiple times while your dog is in position, before asking them to stand back up. Gradually increase how long you pause between rewards, to increase the duration.

(continued)

Lure down and back into a full bow position.

BOW (CONTINUED)

4. Fade out the lure by luring with an empty hand in a sweeping downward motion, gradually doing so farther from your dog's nose. Optionally, you can start a cue transfer by leaning toward your dog as if you are bowing to them before luring. Eventually, the lean can become the cue for this trick.

5. Add a verbal cue, such as "ta-da" or "curtsy," before giving your physical cue.

TIP: If your dog lies down or backs up when you lure them, you are likely luring too far or too quickly. Slow down and focus on rewarding incremental progress toward bowing.

BAR METHOD

MATERIALS

- Bar (broom handle, golf club, pool noodle)
- Two objects to prop up bar (cones with holes, books)

STEPS

1. Set up a horizontal bar at about three-quarters of your dog's height and position your dog to face it in a standing position. Reach under the bar from the side opposite your dog and lure them to duck their head under it. Mark and reward when their head is under the bar, then quickly reset by tossing a second treat behind them or handing them another treat above the bar to prevent them from lying all the way down.

2. Gradually progress from your dog simply ducking their head under the bar, to them crouching into a full bow position. Go slow and be precise with your timing, to help prevent your dog from lying down.

Lure your dog to crouch under the bar.

3. Build duration by rewarding multiple times while your dog is in the bow position, gradually increasing how long you wait in between rewarding, to teach your dog to hold the position.

4. Fade out the lure by luring without a treat in hand, transitioning toward a sweeping downward hand signal. Begin pairing a verbal cue, such as "ta-da!" before giving your hand signal.

5. Raise the bar higher, continuing to cue your dog to bow until you can remove the bar completely. Keep the cones as an environmental cue at first, then finally remove those as well.

ROLL OVER

Stop, drop, and roll over! While your dog doesn't have to master "Play Dead" (page 50) before learning to roll over, this trick is essentially an extension of it. Because of this, a common issue when teaching "Roll Over" to a dog that already knows "Play Dead" is that the dog ends up rolling completely over every time! You can mitigate this by having unique verbal and visual cues for each trick and intentionally practicing distinguishing between them. Alternatively, you could teach these two tricks in opposite directions (e.g., "Play Dead" is always to the right; "Roll Over" is always to the left), to help keep each trick distinct.

As with "Play Dead," be sure to train on a comfortable surface. Never physically grab your dog and turn them over. Rather, take your time with luring this trick to help them build up the muscles needed to roll over.

FOUNDATIONS

- Down (page 23)
- Play Dead (page 50)—optional; you don't have to master it before "Roll Over," but they're taught the same way

STEPS

1. Follow steps 1–3 of the "Play Dead" tutorial.
2. Once your dog will turn onto their side, continue luring in an arc over their body until they roll completely over. This may take many repetitions and approximations; be patient and work at your dog's pace! Continue until your dog will fluidly roll over when you lure them.
3. Fade the lure into a hand signal by luring without a treat. Motion more subtly until your dog will roll in response to you circling your hand in front of them. Add a verbal cue, such as "roll over," before signaling.

PRAY

If my dog could actually say her prayers, I can guarantee she would ask for two things: a refrigerator full of cheese and a yard full of squirrels! "Pray" is an adorable trick in which your dog places their front paws on an object and ducks their head between them. You could also call this trick "duck and cover" or "hide your eyes!"

You can teach this trick either by having your dog put their front paws up on an object, such as a chair, or on your arm. If your dog isn't familiar with putting their paws on your arm, you can build that skill by cueing "Shake" (page 27) while you hold out your arm instead of your hand. Then, use a treat to lure your dog up and forward until they lift their other paw onto your arm as well.

FOUNDATIONS

- Front Paws Up (page 30)

MATERIALS

- Chair, couch, or stool (optional)

STEPS

1. Cue your dog to put their front paws up on your arm or a stable surface that is just above their shoulder height. Slowly move a treat up and down in front of them, rewarding them for keeping their paws up. You aren't luring your dog yet—you are just teaching them to stay in position even if you are moving a treat around.

2. Reach your hand between your dog's front paws from below. Lure your dog's head down through their paws, marking and rewarding when they dip their head down. If they take their paws off to follow the treat, go back to step 1 and slowly work your way toward being able to do this step.

Lure your dog's head down between their paws.

3. Lure as in step 2, but pause with the treat just out of reach before marking and rewarding, to encourage your dog to hold the position. Gradually increase the duration.

4. Fade out the lure by repeating steps 2 and 3 with an empty hand. Then, lure from farther away until you can cue with just a swipe down in front of your dog rather than reaching under their paws.

5. Add a verbal cue, by saying it before giving your hand signal.

BACK UP

"Back Up" is not only an entertaining trick; it's also very practical! If you need your dog to move out of the way, asking them to back up is more considerate than physically moving them. When done correctly, "Back Up" is also a great skill to use in canine fitness programs or as part of a warm-up before high intensity activities.

One of the biggest challenges with this trick is teaching your dog to back up independently. Many people will start training "Back Up" by simply stepping toward their dog, using spatial pressure to push them to step backward. This method can be uncomfortable for some dogs, and it also makes it very difficult to transition to your dog backing up without you moving into their "bubble." There are various other ways to teach "Back Up;" this method uses "Rear Foot Target" (page 33).

FOUNDATIONS

- Rear Foot Target (page 33)

MATERIALS

- Platform
- Flat target (yoga mat, towel, foam mat)

STEPS

1. Practice a few repetitions of cueing "Rear Foot Target," with your dog walking forward over the platform, then cue several reps until your dog steps back to place their feet on the target. This skill is already a strong start to backing up!
2. Gradually increase the distance your dog has to step backward to reach the target, by rewarding from farther ahead between repetitions. Continue to increase the distance until they can walk backward several feet (about 80 cm) to the target.
3. Begin adding a verbal cue, such as "back!" or "beep," as they step back. You can also add a hand signal, such as flicking your fingers toward your dog as if "shooing" them away.
4. Transition from using a platform that is a few inches high to a flat target. Continue to practice steps 2 and 3, using this new target, lowering your criteria at first before increasing the distance again.
5. Take away the target and cue your dog to back up. Try switching between repetitions with and without a target at first. Practice in many different settings to help generalize this skill.

TIP: To help your dog back up straight, position them initially with a wall on one side and another barrier on the other side.

CRAWL

When teaching your dog to crawl, it's fitting that you need to work at a snail's pace! Slicing this trick into small approximations and going slow makes a huge difference in helping your dog understand the goal of "army crawling" on their belly. Plan to practice this trick over many training sessions, and you will see progress before you know it!

Some dogs will prefer to do this trick on extra-soft surfaces, such as plush carpet, whereas others will do better on a smooth rug or cushioned mats. Avoid hard surfaces, such as tile or wood, which can be uncomfortable for your dog. Make the adjustments your dog needs to be successful.

FOUNDATIONS

- Down (page 23)

STEPS

1. With a few treats in hand, cue your dog to lie down. Reward several times while they are down, to reinforce remaining in that position rather than standing back up.
2. Hold a treat at your dog's nose and slowly drag your hand forward along the floor. Mark and reward any movement forward; for example, your dog may only stretch their neck out or move a paw or two at first. Progress until your dog can crawl one or more full steps.
3. Gradually increase how many steps your dog takes before you reward until they can crawl several body lengths. Up your expectations very gradually, only asking your dog to crawl farther when they have consistently been successful with the previous criteria.
4. Lure your dog to crawl with an empty hand. Reduce your distance expectations temporarily, then work back up to crawling farther.
5. Fade the lure to a hand signal by shaking your fist while luring. After many repetitions, cue with this shaking motion a few inches from your dog's nose, so that they crawl toward you. Increase the distance you cue from over time, and add a verbal cue, such as "crawl."

TIP: If your dog stands or lifts their rear end rather than crawling flat, lure slowly and progress in tiny, achievable increments. If they continue to struggle, try luring them under a chair or your legs.

BRAIN BREAK

SNIFFY ADVENTURE

Almost nothing beats the benefits of taking your dog for a walk where they're allowed to sniff, sniff, sniff! Sometimes called a "decompression walk," "sniffari," or just a "sniffy walk," the key characteristic of this type of outing is allowing your dog the freedom to move and smell wherever they please.

Compared to the more traditional picture of walking a dog that involves a brisk pace and a short leash, sniffy walks provide a wealth of benefits for your dog's well-being. Sniffing engages your dog's brain, helps lower their heart rate, and has an overall calming effect. In addition to sniffing, this type of walk also allows your dog to engage in other natural behaviors that are crucial for giving them an enriched life—running, digging, rolling, and simply being a dog!

If you find your dog seems restless before or after training (or at any other time), a sniffy walk may be just what they need to feel contented!

Tips for a successful sniffy adventure:

- **Choose the right spot.** Nature-filled locations, such as wooded trails, beaches, or open fields, provide your dog with endless new things to sniff. If you don't have access to those places, dog-friendly sport fields or other empty grassy areas are also great options. Although neighborhoods are typically busier than ideal for a stress-free walk, you can still allow your dog extra freedom to sniff in more suburban and urban areas, to reap some benefits. Try to visit a variety of places, to keep things exciting for your dog!
- **Use a long leash.** A standard 6-foot (2 m) leash doesn't allow your dog very much space to explore. Try using a longer, lightweight leash (I like to use a leash that's 20 feet [about 6 m] or longer), to give your dog more room to roam.
- **Ask little of your dog.** Sniffy walks are not the time to extensively practice heeling, call your dog back to you a thousand times, or ask them to perform countless tricks. It's your dog's time to do what they want to do! Only ask your dog to do what is necessary (e.g., calling them to you when passing people or other animals), reward them generously, and promptly release them back to sniffing when possible. Practicing a few repetitions of crucial skills, such as returning to you, to keep skills sharp, is fine, but don't overdo it!
- **Practice patience.** It's easy to become antsy and want to move on when your dog is pausing to sniff a single tree for several minutes. Avoid the temptation to ask them to move on and instead use the time to take some deep breaths, relax, and enjoy time with them in nature. It can be just as beneficial for you as it is for your dog!

THE MODEL DOG

There is one universal truth about all dog parents: Your camera roll is filled to the brim with pictures of your pup. You likely have thousands of photos of your dog snoozing, acting silly, or embarking on adventures with you. In this chapter, we'll teach your dog a handful of tricks to help them be camera-ready. These tricks are perfect for capturing memories with your best friend that go beyond basic poses like "Sit" and "Down." Post your snapshots on social media, set them as your phone wallpaper, or hang them up on the wall; however you choose to share them, these eye-catching tricks are picture-perfect!

WAVE

Teaching your dog to wave their paw is an adorable way for them to say "hello" to you and new people they meet! If you can be quick with your camera, it's also a dynamic pose to capture for a photo. "Wave" can be taught as a simple extension of "Shake" (page 27) and many dogs catch on to it quickly.

Once your dog learns to wave with one paw, you can teach them a separate cue for waving with the other paw. Your dog will need a solid foundation of "Shake" with each paw, so revisit that tutorial if needed. Use a distinctive verbal cue for each paw and use the corresponding hand to signal.

FOUNDATIONS

- Shake (page 27)

STEPS

1. Cue your dog to "Shake," holding your hand a little bit higher every few repetitions. Progress until your dog can reach their paw at or above their shoulder height to touch your hand. Switch to holding your hand in an upright "high-five" position rather than in a downward "handshake" position.
2. Cue a high-five and pull your hand away just before your dog's paw touches your hand. Mark when they reach their paw out toward you and reward.
3. Gradually reach your hand out less so that your dog waves their paw in the air.
4. Introduce a hand signal by waving your hand as you reach toward your dog. After many repetitions, try waving your hand without reaching toward your dog. Jackpot when they lift their paw!
5. Add a verbal cue, such as "wave" or "say hi," before giving your hand signal.

CROSS PAWS

Feeling fancy? Teach your dog to pose by crossing one paw over the other! This trick is charming in action and perfect for snapping a portrait. As with "Wave" (page 68), you can build on "Shake" (page 27) to teach your dog this trick. The key is to progress slowly so they learn to move only one paw while keeping the other still.

Take this trick a step further by repeating the process to teach your dog to cross the other paw. It's helpful if they already have a strong foundation of "Shake" with each paw. Use a separate cue for each paw; using "criss-" and "-cross" is a cute way to cue your dog to cross one paw, then the other!

FOUNDATIONS

- Shake (page 27)

MATERIALS

- Small target (coaster, food storage lid, collapsible water bowl)

STEPS

1. With your dog lying down, cue "Shake." After a few repetitions with the same paw, hold a small target in your palm and cue "Shake" again. Mark and reward when your dog paws the target.

2. Move the target slightly toward the opposite paw and cue "Shake." Mark and reward when your dog hits the target with the correct paw.

Move the target across your dog's other paw.

3. Continue moving the target farther across the other paw in small increments, only progressing once your dog is consistently hitting the target with the correct paw at the previous position. Crossing your hand from one side to the other will become the hand signal for this trick, so deliberately move the target into position before cueing "Shake."

(continued)

CROSS PAWS (CONTINUED)

4. Once your dog can cross one paw all the way over the other, place the target on the floor where you want their paw to land. Move your hand across and cue your dog to tap the target. Jackpot!

5. Remove the target and gesture across to cue your dog to cross their paw. Add a verbal cue, such as "cross" or "fancy," before your hand signal!

TIP: If your dog starts hitting the target with the wrong paw, you may be moving it too far, too fast. Practice more repetitions with the target directly in front of the paw you want your dog to use, and move it across their other paw in minute increments as they're successful.

PEEKABOO

"Peekaboo" is the perfect trick to showcase the bond between you and your dog! In this trick, your dog goes behind you and ends standing between your legs. Capture a close-up of your dog in the middle position from your point of view, or have a friend snap a head-to-toe picture of you and your dog for the perfect photo!

Not only is this trick great for photos, but it's also very practical. In crowded settings where you want to keep your dog close to you, asking them to sit or stand between your legs is a great way to keep them safe and out of the way. "Peekaboo" is also the foundation for one of my favorite tricks, "Footsies" (page 155)!

STEPS

1. Start with your dog in front of you and a treat in each hand. With your left hand, lure them around the outside of your left leg. Reward from your left hand when your dog begins to wrap around the back of your leg.
2. Immediately pick up the luring motion with your right hand, reaching between your legs from the front, to guide your dog to stand between your legs. Mark and reward while they are still in position.
3. Fade out the first half of the lure. Sweep your left hand to the side to send your dog around your leg, then lure them with a treat into the final position.

(continued)

PEEKABOO (CONTINUED)

4. Fade out the second lure until your dog automatically stops in the middle when you cue with just your outside hand.
5. Add a verbal cue, such as "peekaboo," "middle," or "center," before giving your hand signal.

NOTE: You can switch the direction of this trick to go around your right side, if you prefer; just switch the directions noted in these steps.

TIP: You can place a target between your feet, to help your dog have a more concrete understanding of where they should stop. Remove the target once your dog catches on.

CHIN REST

If you don't like having your picture taken but still want some photos of you and your dog together, then "Chin Rest" is a fantastic option for capturing memories! In this trick, your dog places their snout flat on your outstretched hand. It's the perfect pose for showcasing their adoring eyes looking up at you!

These steps explore how to lure this trick. You could instead teach this trick through shaping by holding your hand palm up in front of your dog and rewarding as they get closer to offering the behavior on their own. Another alternative option is to start with "Touch" (page 24), then slowly flip the positioning of your hand to build a chin rest.

STEPS

1. Hold your hand, palm up, in front of your dog just below their chin level. With the other hand, lure their nose over your hand, moving the treat down slightly until their chin rests on your hand. Mark and reward while your dog's chin is still in your hand.

2. Build duration by holding the treat just beyond your dog's reach while their muzzle rests on your hand, gradually increasing how long you pause before rewarding.

3. Fade out the lure by holding out your flat palm, then motioning as in steps 1 and 2, but without a treat in hand. Gradually decrease how much you lure after holding out your hand.

4. Hold out your palm and pause before luring. Jackpot if your dog places their snout in your palm!

5. Add a verbal cue, such as "chin" or "rest," before giving your hand signal.

TIP: If your dog knows "Shake" (page 27) and automatically puts their paw in your hand when you hold out your palm, you could teach them to do a chin rest on just a few fingers or on your lap!

BOOP

Boop (verb)—to gently and affectionately tap a dog on the nose.

In this trick, your dog will stick their perfectly boopable nose through your hands held in the shape of a heart or circle. For smaller dogs, you can hold just one hand in an O shape, rather than using both hands. To take the cutest photos of this trick, have a helper take pictures over your shoulder or prop up your phone to record a video from your point of view. Once your dog gets the hang of this trick, try variations, such as holding your hand in the shape of different letters (e.g., L-O-V-E) and snap photos to spell out a word!

TOUCH METHOD

FOUNDATIONS

- Touch (page 24)

STEPS

1. Practice a few repetitions of cueing "Touch."
2. Transition from cueing "Touch" with a flat palm to holding your hand in a C shape. Mark and reward when your dog touches your hand, even if they aren't sticking their nose through the middle yet.
3. Shift the position of your hand until your dog sticks their nose through the middle of the C. Jackpot!
4. Add a new verbal cue, such as "boop" or "snoot," before your dog sticks their nose through.
5. Slowly add your other hand to create a circle or heart shape and say your cue.

LURING METHOD

STEPS

1. Hold one hand in a C shape and use a treat in your other hand to lure your dog's nose through the C. Mark and reward while their nose is still resting in your hand.
2. Repeat step 1 without a treat: hold up your C hand, then lure your dog through. Motion more subtly over time to fade out the lure.
3. Add your verbal cue once your dog will poke their nose through when you just hold up your C hand. Say "boop" or "snoot," then hold up your hand.
4. Slowly add your other hand to create a circle or heart shape, and say your cue.

(continued)

BOOP (CONTINUED)

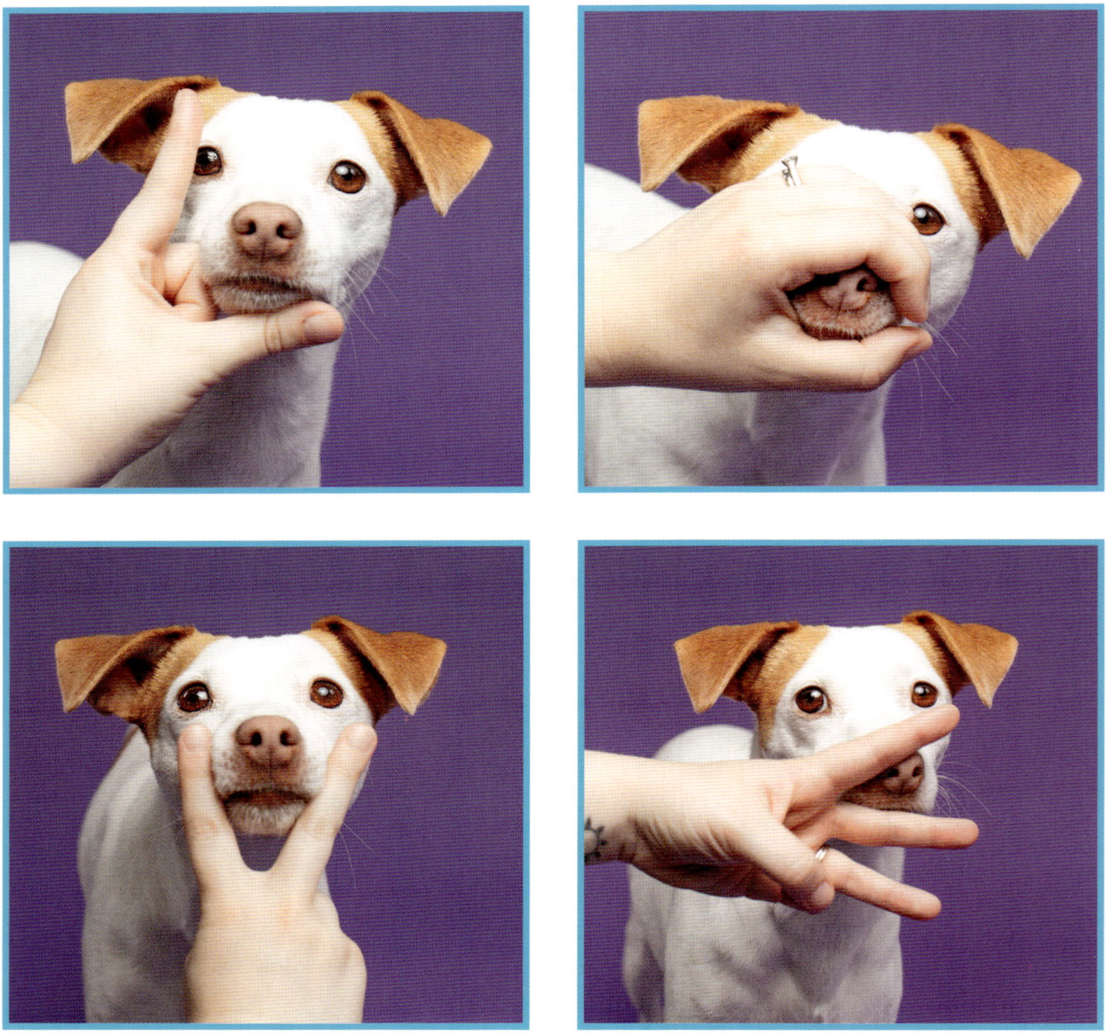

Try holding your hand in different shapes to spell out a word, such as L-O-V-E!

HEAD DOWN

"Head Down" is one of the most endearing tricks for photos. When your dog lays their head flat on the ground or another surface, it creates the sweetest and most innocent-looking expression! Only teach this trick if you want your camera to be full of adorable photos of your pup (and who doesn't want that?).

There are a few approaches to teaching this trick. You could shape the trick by starting with your dog lying down and rewarding as they naturally dip their head until it is flat on the floor or on an object placed in front of them. You can also build this skill starting with the trick "Chin Rest" (page 77), or by luring.

CHIN REST METHOD

FOUNDATIONS

- Down (page 23)
- Chin Rest (page 77)

STEPS

1. With your dog lying down, practice a few repetitions of cueing "Chin Rest."
2. Gradually lower your hand toward the floor every few repetitions, until your hand is resting on the floor. Reward from your other hand while your dog is still resting their head on your hand.
3. Begin to create a hand signal by sweeping your hand down into position before cueing the chin rest.
4. Fade out the hand target by gradually pulling your hand away before your dog rests their chin on it. Jackpot once their chin makes any contact with the floor!

5. Once your dog will rest their chin on the floor in front of your hand, add a new verbal cue, such as "head down," before giving your hand signal.

(continued)

LURING METHOD

FOUNDATIONS

- Down (page 23)

MATERIALS

- Towel or pillow

STEPS

1. Ask your dog to lie down and place a folded-up towel or pillow in front of them. Lure your dog's head down and forward, until their chin rests on the object. Mark and reward while your dog's head is still down.

2. Build duration by holding the treat out of their reach for a moment before rewarding.

3. Transition toward your dog doing this behavior on the floor, by switching to a smaller pillow/towel or unfolding the towel a bit at a time. Progress until your dog will rest their head on a flat towel.

4. Remove the towel target and lure the behavior. Jackpot if your dog rests their head on the ground!

5. Fade the lure into a hand signal by sweeping your hand down without a treat. Add a verbal cue, such as "head down," before giving your hand signal.

Lure your dog's head onto a pillow or towel.

KISS

My dog's favorite activity in the world is licking me for as long as I will let her; no training was needed for that! For some less exuberant affection, teach your dog to give you a "kiss" on the cheek. In this version of the trick, they will give you a "peck" with their nose instead of actually licking you . . . though, if your dog is like mine, they may still try to sneak in a lick anyway!

"Kiss" is an extension of "Touch" (page 24). If your dog knows "Touch" well, they have a great foundation for this trick already. Once your dog masters "Kiss," try capturing a selfie of your dog giving you a smooch for a sweet photo!

FOUNDATIONS

- Touch (page 24)

STEPS

1. Practice a few repetitions of cueing "Touch" to your hand.
2. Continue to cue "Touch," moving your hand closer to your cheek every few repetitions until it's resting on your face. Lean your face toward your dog before asking them to touch, to start building this as a cue.
3. Fade out your hand target by placing just a few fingers on your cheek when cueing "Touch," progressing until your dog will touch their nose to just one finger pointed at your cheek.
4. Add a verbal cue, such as "kiss," before leaning in and pointing to your cheek.
5. Try giving your verbal cue and leaning toward your dog without pointing as an additional cue. Jackpot if they give you a "kiss" on the cheek!

TELL ME A SECRET

If your dog could tell you a secret, would they confess to stealing your socks? Or would they just tell you that you're their favorite person in the world (but that's not a secret, right)? In this trick, you'll teach your dog to put their nose to your ear to "spill the tea!"

Like "Kiss" (page 85), this trick is a dressed-up version of "Touch" (page 24). To make this trick extra entertaining, be sure to act surprised when your dog tells you their secret. This creates the perfect storytelling moment to capture in a photo or video!

FOUNDATIONS

- Touch (page 24)

STEPS

1. Practice cueing "Touch" to your hand while your dog is at your side. You can have them sit or stand on a small platform to help them stay in place, if needed.
2. Continue to cue "Touch," gradually moving your hand closer to your ear every few repetitions until your dog will touch their nose to your hand while you cup your ear.
3. Build duration by gradually increasing how long you wait before rewarding or cueing the trick a second time before rewarding. Have a treat ready in your off hand, so that you can quickly reach up and reward while your dog is still in the "secret" position, to help encourage duration.
4. Add a verbal cue, such as "tell me a secret!" or "spill the tea," before cueing with your hand.

TIP: Instead of using "Touch," you could build this trick off "Chin Rest" (page 77), slowly transitioning toward cupping your hand as in these steps.

TAKE A SELFIE

A section about picture-perfect tricks wouldn't be complete without the ultimate dog trick for your camera roll—taking a selfie! For this trick, your dog will put their front paws up on your shoulder(s) and look up at the camera. You can take a real selfie using this trick, or use this pose for a fun portrait of you and your pup!

This trick is very adaptable; you can teach your dog to put one paw on each shoulder, both paws on one side, or just one paw on your shoulder. Smaller dogs may need to sit on a platform or chair behind you, to be tall enough to reach. Alternatively, you can teach your dog to place their chin on your shoulder, using methods similar to "Chin Rest" (page 77) or "Head Down" (page 81).

FOUNDATIONS

- Front Paws Up (page 30)

MATERIALS

- Platform or chair (optional)

STEPS

1. Cue "Front Paws Up" on your arm. If your dog is unfamiliar with putting their paws on your arm, try cueing "Shake" (see page 27) while holding out your forearm to your dog, then use a treat to lure them forward and up until they lift their other paw to your arm.
2. Position your dog behind you (you can use a platform or chair to help them stay in place). Cue "Front Paws Up" on your shoulder rather than your arm. For larger dogs, duck your head down and cue "Front Paws Up" toward the center of your shoulders, so that your dog places a paw on each side. Use a treat to help lure your dog, if needed.
3. Start a cue transfer by lifting your phone to take a "selfie" before cueing "Front Paws Up." Your dog should begin to anticipate what you will ask them to do next after you raise your phone, creating a new cue for this trick.
4. Hold up your phone and pause before cueing "Front Paws Up." Jackpot if your dog puts their paws up!
5. Add a verbal cue, such as "selfie," before holding up your phone.

TIP: To get your dog to look at the camera, try holding a treat in the same hand as your phone and reward from that hand. Or you could even clip a treat pouch to your phone!

BRAIN BREAK

HIDE-AND-TREAT

We talked about the incredible benefits of sniffing in the "Sniffy Adventure" brain break (page 64). A simple activity that can engage your dog in sniffing and exploring indoors is playing a game of "Hide-and-Treat!" Hiding treats around a room gives your dog the chance to activate their natural seeking system as they scavenge for food, which provides excellent enrichment to help them feel more relaxed and satisfied. Follow these simple steps to set up this activity for your dog:

1. Hide a treat (smelly treats work great for this!) in an easy spot while your dog watches, then release them to get the treat. You can place treats directly on the floor or use small, open containers.
2. Work up to hiding multiple treats in progressively more challenging spots, still allowing your dog to watch as they learn the game.
3. With your dog waiting out of sight, hide a few treats in easy locations. Release your dog to sniff out the treats. Allow them time to search for the treats on their own, but give them some guidance (or try an easier spot next time) if they're struggling.
4. Once your dog learns the game, hide more treats in a wider search area and in more challenging spots for them to seek out.

BONUS: For another twist on this game, hide puzzle toys filled with treats (or your dog's meal!) around the house, for an extra-challenging scavenger hunt.

THE HELPER DOG

From herding sheep to tracking scents, dogs are no strangers to having jobs. While your average canine companion may not carry out a bona fide job on a daily basis, they can still learn to perform some "chores" at home! After all, who couldn't use an extra set of hands (or rather, paws) around the house? This chapter lays out how to teach your dog several tricks that mimic "helping" you around the house in an entertaining, light-hearted manner. Be sure to compensate your dog fairly with lots of treats for their hard work!

OPEN A DOOR

If your dog loves to tug, then opening doors is the perfect job for them! This trick requires them to pull on a rope to swing a door open. For smaller dogs, cabinet or dog crate doors work well. Taller dogs can open unlatched standard doors or even a fridge door!

This trick is also the first step in teaching some advanced multistep, or "chain," behaviors. For example, you could teach your dog to open the fridge, fetch a bottle from it, then close the door. You could also teach your dog to open their kennel door, go inside, then pull the door shut. This trick "opens the door" for so many other tricks!

FOUNDATIONS

- Tug (page 38)

MATERIALS

- Rope or length of strong fabric (braided strips of an old shirt or tall sock)
- Outward-opening door with a handle

STEPS

1. Practice cueing "Tug" with the rope, not attached to the door yet, while holding it in your hand like a toy.
2. Attach the rope to the door handle. Grab the rope and cue "Tug," holding tight so that the door doesn't move at first. After several repetitions, allow the door to open slowly as your dog pulls.
3. Gradually loosen your hold on the rope so your dog begins to open the door on their own. Avoid letting the door open too quickly, until your dog is confident.
4. Transition to pointing toward the rope, rather than holding it, and cue your dog to tug the door open.
5. Add a new verbal cue, such as "open it," before gesturing for your dog to pull the door open. Practice cueing from farther away, to make this trick more independent.

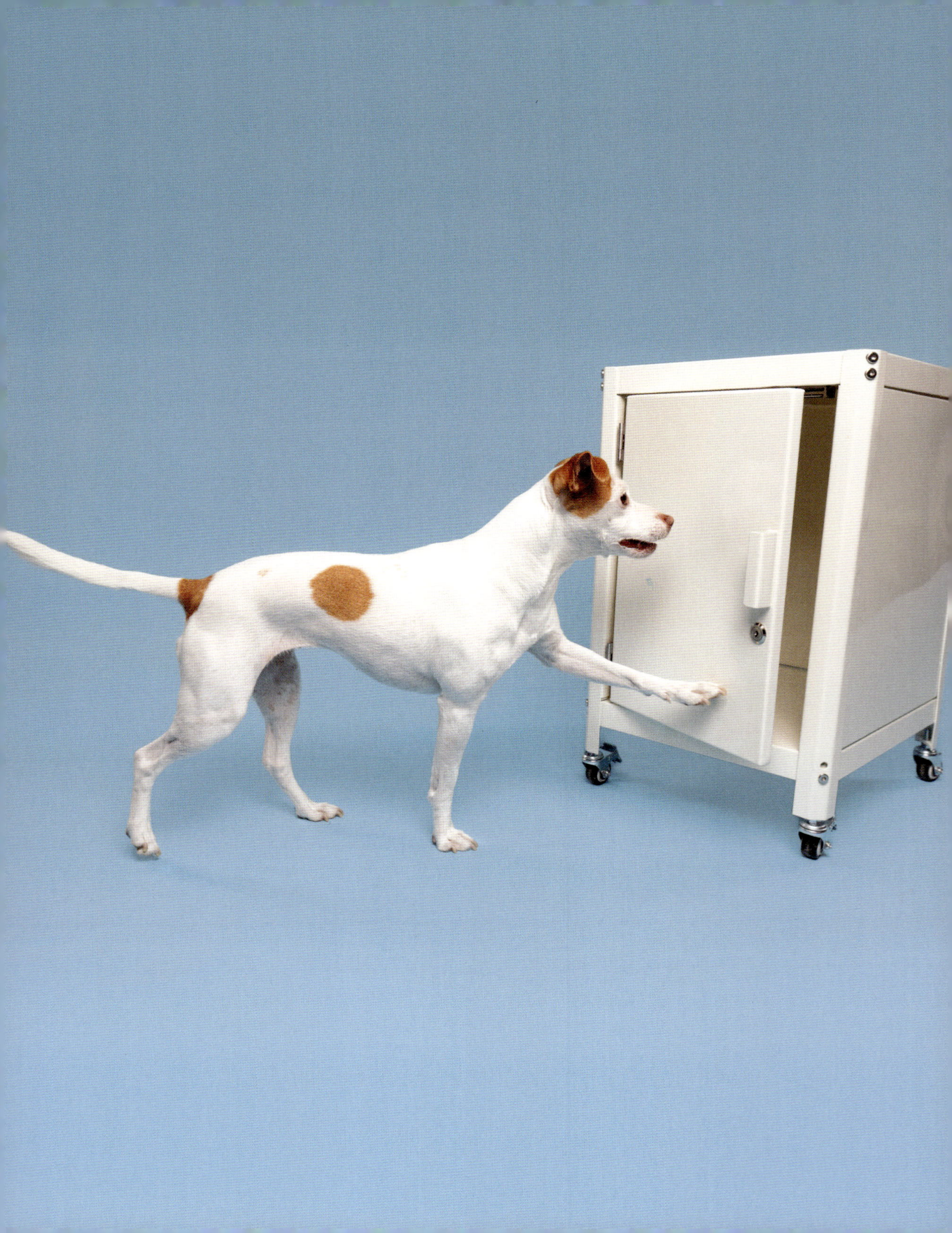

CLOSE A DOOR

The perfect way for your dog to lend a paw is by closing a door for you! This trick builds off a paw target learned through "Shake" (page 27). Alternatively, you could teach this trick building off "Touch" (page 24), or by cueing "Front Paws Up" (page 30) on the vertical surface of a tall door.

Cabinet, standard, and even fridge doors can all work well for this trick. If asking your dog to close a door that slams loudly, drape a towel over the top or cut a pool noodle to fit over the side, to avoid startling them. Depending on your dog's comfort level, you may be able to remove the buffer eventually.

FOUNDATIONS

- Shake (page 27)

MATERIALS

- Sticky note
- Door

STEPS

1. Practice a few repetitions of cueing "Shake." Then, hold a sticky note in your palm and cue "shake" again, marking and rewarding as your dog paws the paper.
2. Hold your hand with the sticky note facing outward against a closed door, and cue "Shake."
3. Attach the paper to the door. Tap the sticky note to cue your dog to paw it, moving your hand away so they hit the paper rather than your hand. Once your dog is consistently pawing at the sticky note, add a new verbal cue, such as "close it," before gesturing.
4. Open the door a crack and cue the behavior. Every few repetitions, open the door a little bit wider.
5. When your dog can paw the door closed with minimal support, remove the sticky note. Gradually increase the distance you cue from, once they get the hang of it!

WIPE YOUR PAWS

After your dog has enjoyed a good romp around in the yard, you let them back inside only to realize . . . their paws are covered in mud! Now the carpet, couch, and even your clothes are covered in mud, too. The solution? Teach your dog how to wipe their paws! Especially for dogs who love to use their paws, this trick is a lot of fun to learn.

Once your dog learns to wipe their paws on a towel or rug, you can transfer this skill to other surfaces. You can ask them to fake "dig" on the carpet or even cue them to dig in the dirt outside. One of my favorite applications is using this trick to teach a dog to scratch a board with sandpaper on it (this is called a scratch board) to file their own nails!

MATERIALS

- Towel or small rug

STEPS

1. Place a treat under a towel and hold the towel down. Wait for your dog to try to get the treat. Immediately mark and reward by uncovering the treat when your dog paws at the towel.

2. Wait for your dog to paw multiple times before rewarding. Tap the top of the towel with a scratching motion before your dog paws it, to start adding a visual cue.

3. Place the towel down without a treat under it and give your hand signal. Jackpot if your dog paws at the towel! Repeat, interspersing repetitions where there is a treat under the towel, to keep your dog engaged.

4. Once your dog can consistently dig without a hidden treat, add a verbal cue, such as "dig" or "wipe your paws," before giving your hand signal. Make your hand signal more subtle by gradually cueing farther above the towel.

Place a treat under the towel.

TIP: If your dog tries to get the treat with their mouth, drape the towel over an upright board. Cue "Shake" near the towel and move your hand away, so your dog paws the towel. Gradually position the board more horizontally.

TAKE OFF MY SHOE

Dogs who learn this trick must think, "Wait, you actually want me to take your shoe?!?" It's every dog's dream! To teach this trick, your dog will need to know how to tug various objects. Using a shoe without a back, such as a slipper or sandal, is typically easiest for your dog. Alternatively, you could teach them to pull off a loose sock instead.

To add an extra element to this trick, try teaching your dog to pull off one shoe, then the other. You could also teach them to hand the shoe to you, using the "Fetch" trick (page 41), or to put it away in a basket, similar to the trick "Clean Up Your Toys" (page 106).

FOUNDATIONS

- Tug (page 38)

MATERIALS

- Shoe (slipper, sandal, or loose sock)

STEPS

1. Hold the shoe in front of your dog and cue "Tug." Wiggle it around like a toy, to make it exciting, until they pull on it.
2. Place the slipper partially on your foot and hold it in your hand, then cue "Tug" again. Mark and reward when your dog tugs on the shoe, working until they can pull it all the way off.
3. With the slipper still only loosely on your foot, hold your foot up to your dog and cue "Tug" without holding the shoe with your hand. Jackpot when they tug it!
4. Work toward putting the slipper fully on your foot, until your dog can pull it off completely.
5. Add a new verbal cue, such as "shoes," before asking your dog to tug the shoe.

TIP: If your dog will not take the shoe in their mouth to tug at first, practice a few repetitions of cueing "Tug" with a familiar toy, then immediately try again with the shoe. Or try this trick with a fluffy sock that resembles a toy!

FETCH A TISSUE

Although you may not be able to teach your dog to say "bless you" when you sneeze, you can teach them to fetch you a tissue! For this trick, you will use a cue transfer to train your dog to bring you a tissue from a box when you say "a-choo!" You may modify the following steps to teach them to pull a fake tissue (e.g., a small towel) out of a box instead. If using an empty box and a rag, try placing a rock or other heavy weight in the bottom to help keep the box in place.

As an extra step, you could also teach your dog to place the used tissue in the trash after you "blow your nose." To do this, follow the same methods as for "Clean Up Your Toys" (page 106), using a small trash can as the target.

FOUNDATIONS

- Fetch (page 41)

MATERIALS

- Tissue box

STEPS

1. Grab a single tissue and encourage your dog to take it in their mouth; you can move it around like a toy, cue "Hold" (see page 37), or even toss it. Work up to cueing them to fetch the tissue off the ground and bring it back to you.
2. Tuck a loose tissue into the opening of the box (this tends to work better than having your dog pull out a tissue that's folded in with the rest) and cue them to take it out. As in step 1, work until your dog can fetch it from the box and bring it to your hand.
3. Place the tissue box incrementally farther from you and cue your dog to fetch the tissue.
4. Add an "a-choo!" cue by doing a fake sneeze into your elbow, covering your nose, then cueing your dog to fetch the tissue.
5. After many repetitions, give your "a-choo!" cue and wait before giving your "Fetch" cue. If your dog brings you the tissue, jackpot! If not, go back to step 4.

FETCH YOUR LEASH

When it's time to go for a walk, your dog can help out by retrieving their own leash! This trick is just a specific version of the trick "Fetch" (page 41). Although some dogs are eager to retrieve anything you ask them to, others may need to get used to holding the leash in their mouth. Try a soft, lightweight, fabric leash to make it easier for your pup.

To add another layer to this trick, place the leash in a low basket and ask your dog to fetch the leash from it. A more challenging option is to drape the leash over a hook; if doing this, you'll need to teach your dog to tug the leash down. Be sure to position the leash so that they pull from the clip side, to prevent that part from flying down and hitting them. My favorite version of this trick is to clip the leash to my dog's harness or collar, drop the leash, then cue her to pick up the leash for me!

FOUNDATIONS

- Fetch (page 41)

MATERIALS

- Dog leash

STEPS

1. Get your dog interested in taking the leash in their mouth. Playfully shake it around, toss it like a toy, or use a generalized cue, such as "Hold" or "Tug."
2. Cue your dog to fetch the leash off the ground. Tossing it at first can make it more like a game! Practice until they will bring the leash to your hand.
3. Gradually increase the distance from which you ask your dog to fetch the leash.
4. Add a verbal cue, such as "get your leash," before cueing your dog to retrieve it.
5. Practice having other items around and cueing your dog to fetch their leash specifically; slowly increase the number of distractor items and reward your dog for fetching the correct item.

CLEAN UP YOUR TOYS

Even if you have a basket (or two) for your dog's toys, you probably end up with more toys scattered around your house than actually in the toy bin. Cleaning up all their toys seems fruitless when you know your dog will take them all out again, so why not teach them to put away their own toys?

If your dog already knows how to fetch, they have a great foundation for this trick. The other key skill your dog will need to learn is to target the basket, rather than your hand, when bringing the toys back. This skill is also important for other tricks that involve putting one object into another, including dunking a basketball into a hoop (see page 129).

FOUNDATIONS

- Fetch (page 41)

MATERIALS

- Toy bin
- Several dog toys

STEPS

1. Use shaping to teach your dog to put their head in the basket: Place a basket between you and your dog, and mark when they interact with the basket (looking at it, sniffing it, etc.). Reward by placing a treat in the basket. Progress until your dog puts their head inside the basket.

2. Practice tossing a toy and using your "Fetch" cue to ask your dog to bring it to your hand. Work toward asking your dog to retrieve a stationary toy. Then, place more than one toy out on the floor and cue "Fetch," working one by one, until all are retrieved.

(continued)

Teach your dog to put their head in the basket.

CLEAN UP YOUR TOYS (CONTINUED)

3. Combine steps 1 and 2. Place the basket between you and your dog, and toss a single toy. Mark and reward if they place it near the basket, even if not inside it at first. Repeat, jackpotting once your dog places the toy in the basket!

4. Work up to asking your dog to fetch a stationary toy to the basket. Add a verbal cue, such as "clean up," before cueing them to retrieve the toy.

5. Place multiple toys around the basket for your dog to clean up. Place toys farther away for an extra challenge!

TIP: If you are having trouble shaping step 1, try tossing treats into the basket, to get your dog interested.

TIP: If your dog needs extra support learning to put the toy in the basket, try holding your hand in or above the basket as they fetch the toy. Move your hand away once your dog learns to target the basket.

TUCK YOURSELF IN

After a long day of "helping" you around the house, it's time for your dog to turn in for the night. Teach them to roll themselves up in a blanket for the perfect bedtime trick! You can also call this trick "burrito" as a fitting name for your dog wrapping themselves up; use a round blanket printed to look like a tortilla to make this version even better!

This trick chains two tricks together: "Hold" (page 37) and "Roll Over" (page 56). To add one final step to this trick, you could also cue "Head Down" (see page 81) after your dog rolls up inside the blanket. This creates the perfect illusion of your dog tucking themselves in for a good sleep!

FOUNDATIONS

- Hold (page 37)
- Roll Over (page 56)

MATERIALS

- Small rag
- Blanket

STEPS

1. Practice a few repetitions of cueing "Hold" with the rag. Cue your dog to do simple tricks while holding it ("Spin," "Sit," "Down," "Shake," etc.). They may drop the rag before performing the second trick at first; reward anyway and keep practicing. Jackpot when they continue to hold the rag while doing another trick!

2. With your dog lying down, cue them to hold the rag. Cue "Roll Over." As in step 1, reward even if they drop the rag before rolling. Continue practicing and jackpot once your dog holds the rag while rolling.

(continued)

TUCK YOURSELF IN (CONTINUED)

3. Place the rag next to your dog on the side they roll away from. Cue them to pick up the rag, then to roll over with it.
4. Cue your dog to lie down toward one end of a blanket. Most of the blanket should be on the side your dog will roll toward, but leave some slack on the side your dog will grab. Pick up the corner of the blanket and ask your dog to hold it, then cue "Roll Over." Reward even if they don't hold it the whole way, practicing until they do!
5. Cue your dog to pick the corner of the blanket up and roll over. Over time, they will begin to anticipate that they should roll over once they pick up the blanket. Add a new cue, such as "burrito," before asking your dog to pick up the blanket to create the final cue for this trick!

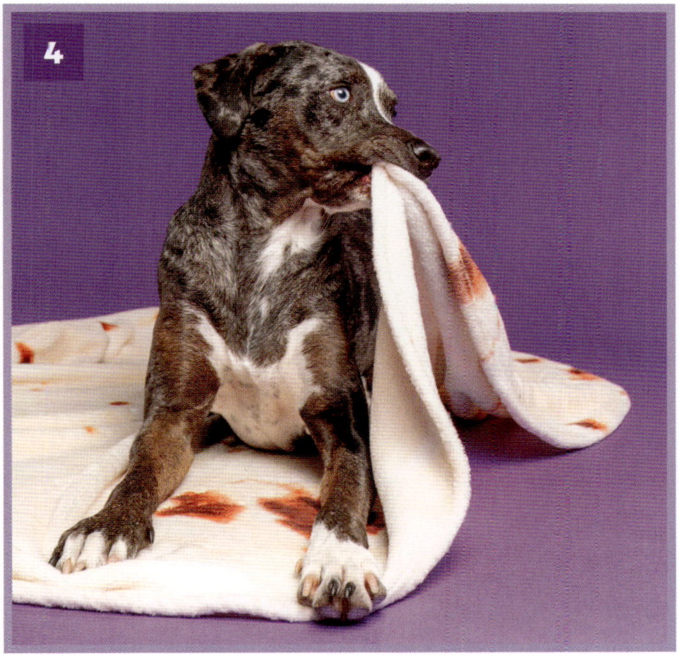

Teach your dog to pick up the blanket before rolling over.

TURN OFF THE LIGHTS

Hey, who turned out the lights? Your dog did! In this trick, you'll teach your dog to turn off a light switch, using their paw. This method uses a battery-operated light switch that you can hold in your hand. For dogs who can reach, you can transfer this skill to a real switch in the end!

If you don't have access to a wireless switch, you could teach this trick exclusively by using a light switch on the wall. Start by teaching your dog to put their front paws on the wall. Then, teach them to paw the switch, using the strategies from "Open a Door" (page 94). This approach is a little simpler if you have a rocker light switch, since they are easier to press, but can be done with toggle switches, too.

FOUNDATIONS

- Shake (page 27)

MATERIALS

- Battery-operated light switch

STEPS

1. Practice a few repetitions of cueing "Shake." Then, hold the light switch in your hand and cue "Shake." Mark and reward when your dog's paw touches the light switch box, even if they don't flip the switch yet.
2. Hold the light switch more vertically and continue rewarding any paw contact with the box. Then, begin waiting for your dog to actually flip the switch down before rewarding. You can start with the switch in a half-flipped position, to make it easier.
3. Once your dog is consistently flipping the switch, mount the light switch to a wood board or wall at your dog's height. Position your hand near the box and cue them to paw the switch.
4. Cue with your hand farther away from the switch until you can cue with just a point. Add a verbal cue, such as "lights out!"

TURN ON THE LIGHTS

Whereas "Turn Off the Lights" (page 112) uses a toggle switch, this trick teaches your dog to turn on a light by using a different prop—a button! Pressing a button is simpler than flipping a switch up, and many dogs catch on after just a few successful repetitions.

The steps for this trick use the trick "Shake" (page 27) to teach your dog to press the button with their paw. Instead, you could modify these steps to build off "Touch" (page 24) to teach your dog to push the button with their nose, either ending with the button on the floor or mounted to the wall. A third option to teach this trick is to simply use shaping: Place the button on the floor in front of your dog, and reward as they figure out to press the button on their own!

FOUNDATIONS

- Shake (page 27)

MATERIALS

- Puck light button

STEPS

1. Practice a few repetitions of cueing "Shake." Then, hold the button in your palm and cue "Shake." Mark and reward when your dog hits the button, even if they don't activate it yet. Continue until your dog presses hard enough to turn on the button, jackpotting when they do!
2. Gradually lower the button until you're holding it on the ground, continuing to cue as in step 1.
3. Set the light on the floor, gesturing to it to encourage your dog to hit it. Jackpot when they press the button on their own.
4. Once your dog is turning on the button on the ground, add a verbal cue, such as "lights on," before pointing toward the button. Practice this trick from a distance, for an extra challenge!

BRAIN BREAK

SHREDDING PALOOZA

Blankets torn to pieces, pillow feathers floating everywhere, socks mangled beyond recognition . . . it's no secret that dogs love to shred! While many dog parents view shredding as a negative, destructive behavior that they need to train their dog to stop entirely, shredding is actually a very natural behavior and can serve as fantastic form of enrichment! Rather than working against nature to eradicate your dog's desire to shred, you can give them appropriate outlets to destroy designated, dog-safe items to satisfy that need. Enrichment that involves shredding can reduce stress and boredom, and it can also help deter your dog from destroying things they shouldn't, since they have opportunities to fulfill their instinct to shred!

After your next training session, try giving your dog some shredding enrichment to enjoy.

Here are some tips to get started:

- Gather dog-safe recyclables: Paper bags, cardboard boxes, packing paper, toilet paper and paper towel tubes, and cardboard egg cartons are great options.
- Hide dry dog food or treats inside the recyclables. Crumple or fold inside paper, dump into boxes and cartons, and pinch the ends of filled tubes closed.
- Supervise your dog as they tear through the materials to find their treats! Make sure your dog isn't consuming anything that's not food. If they seem frustrated or unable to get the food out, try making the game easier by packing the food more loosely.
- If your dog is an expert shredder, increase the challenge by creating layers (e.g., put balled-up packing paper filled with food inside a cardboard egg carton, inside a box). Throw in some easy-to-access treats within the layers to keep your dog motivated!
- For an added layer of enrichment, hide multiple shredding items around the room for your dog to seek out, then destroy!

THE HOBBY DOG

If your dog could pick some human hobbies, what would they do in their free time? Would they join a basketball team, play in a band, create works of art, or travel abroad? Whatever pastime your pup would choose, there's a trick for that! In this chapter, we will teach your dog tricks using entertaining sports, music, and other hobby-themed props. Yard sales and thrift stores are great places to pick up some of these toys to use in your training. If you're ready for your dog to be the next Air Bud, then these tricks are the perfect place to start!

UNROLL A YOGA MAT

Breathe in, breathe out, and teach your dog to do some yoga! These steps use treat placement to teach your dog to unroll a yoga mat with their nose, but alternatively, you could transfer a "Touch" cue (see page 24) or use shaping to build this skill instead. For another variation of this trick, try using a roll of wrapping paper instead of a yoga mat.

A great extension of this trick is to teach your dog to do a "yoga pose," such as "Bow" (page 53) on the mat after unrolling it. Practice many repetitions of cueing "Bow" on the yoga mat, then add for them to unroll the mat beforehand. Through many repetitions, your dog can automatically chain these two tricks together. For an extra cute spin, unroll your own yoga mat next to your dog and do a "downward dog" together!

MATERIALS

- Yoga mat

STEPS

1. Tuck a treat under the rolled-up portion of a yoga mat. Your dog will naturally nudge the roll forward when they retrieve the treat. Mark when they nose the mat and reward by placing another treat on the mat ahead of your dog.
2. Sequence multiple repetitions of step 1 together by immediately placing another treat under the roll each time that your dog pushes the mat. Repeat until they unroll the entire mat.

(continued)

Tuck a treat under the yoga mat.

UNROLL A YOGA MAT (CONTINUED)

3. Fade out the treats by just tapping the roll rather than placing a treat under it on the first repetition. Mark and reward by placing a treat under the roll for the next repetition. Repeat this pattern until your dog unrolls the entire mat.

4. Tap the roll once and wait for your dog to push the roll multiple times in a row before rewarding. Progress until they can unroll the entire mat on one cue.

5. Transition to just pointing toward the yoga mat rather than tapping and add a verbal cue, such as "yoga" or "unroll it," before your dog starts to unroll the mat.

TIP: Instead of tucking one treat at a time under the mat, you could roll several treats inside the mat and allow your dog to unroll the mat to get the treats. After many repetitions, try placing the mat in front of your dog without treats inside, and jackpot from your treat pouch when they unroll the mat!

PAINT A PICTURE

Discover whether your dog is a natural artist by teaching them to paint a picture! For this art lesson, you'll teach your dog to take a brush from your hand, paint a few strokes, then give the brush back to you. This is a challenging trick, but if you take the time to practice the individual steps, your dog will be ready to create a masterpiece in no time.

When preparing your supplies, choose a nontoxic, washable paint and cover the floor to avoid a mess. The handle of a regular brush can be challenging for dogs to hold steadily, so try sticking the brush inside a piece of a pool noodle or foam mat, to create a wide, grippy handle for your dog. Use a small easel or attach the paper/canvas to a wall, to create the perfect painting spot.

FOUNDATIONS

- Hold (page 37)
- Touch (page 24)

MATERIALS

- Paper or canvas
- Paintbrush
- Nontoxic, washable paint

STEPS

1. Cue your dog to "Hold" the brush (no paint yet), then drop it in your hand. Ask them to "Touch" your hand while they're holding the brush. Practice until your dog can hold the brush, touch it to your hand several times in different positions, then drop it into your hand.

(continued)

Teach your dog to touch the brush to your hand.

PAINT A PICTURE (CONTINUED)

2. Set the brush aside and teach your dog to target the paper with their nose. You could use shaping to reward approximations toward touching the paper, or you could hold your hand or a target stick in front of the paper and cue "Touch," fading out your target as your dog learns to target the paper.

3. Combine the skills from steps 1 and 2. With your dog facing the paper, cue them to hold the dry paintbrush, then cue them to touch the paper. Reward any effort, even if they drop the brush at first. Practice until your dog can touch the paper with the brush without letting go, then release the brush into your hand.

4. Teach your dog to make paint strokes, by cueing them to touch the brush to the paper multiple times in a row. You can use a target to help guide them to touch the bottom of the paper, then move up, to make stroke motions.

5. Finally, dip the brush in some paint before handing it to your dog, then create a masterpiece! Add a cue, such as "paint," before asking them to touch the brush to the paper, to create a new verbal cue for this trick.

Teach your dog to touch the paper with their nose.

PLAY SOCCER

She shoots; she scores! The crowd goes wild! Train your dog to be the world's next soccer superstar by teaching them to roll a ball into a goal with their nose. You can adjust the difficulty of this trick by modifying how far your dog must push the ball to reach the goal.

For this trick, you will need a ball and a goal. You can use a soccer ball or any toy ball, ideally one that's larger than your dog can pick up. For the goal, you can go all out and buy a miniature net, or you can simply use a cardboard box or plastic bin that you already have.

MATERIALS

- Ball
- Small goal (toy soccer goal, cardboard box, plastic bin)

STEPS

1. Use shaping to teach your dog to push the ball. Place the ball in front of them and mark and reward for any interaction with it. Begin to focus on rewarding only when they interact with it with their nose, jackpotting once they finally "boop" it forward.
2. Progress until your dog can nose touch the ball multiple times in a row to move it forward. Reward by placing a treat by the ball, to reinforce their keeping their nose near it.
3. Introduce a goal by placing it just behind the ball, so that your dog will naturally push it in. Jackpot when the ball goes in the goal.
4. Gradually move the goal farther away as your dog is successful at pushing the ball in.
5. Add a verbal cue, such as "score," before placing the ball down or gesturing for your dog to nudge the ball.

TIP: If you are struggling with shaping step 1, hold the ball in your hand and cue "Touch" (see page 24) several times. Then, place the ball on the floor and resume shaping, prompting your dog by cueing "Touch," if needed.

PLAY BASKETBALL

Get ready for a slam dunk! For the canine version of basketball, your dog will learn how to pick up a ball and drop it through a hoop. Like the trick "Clean Up Your Toys" (page 106), the foundation of this trick is teaching your dog to target the basket with their nose. Once they have that skill down, it'll be nothing but net!

To teach this trick, you will need a ball that your dog can hold in their mouth and a dog-sized hoop. The hoop can be a children's basketball hoop, an over-the-door hoop hung at your dog's height, or even just a trash can! Position the hoop at your dog's shoulder height for more of a challenge, or make it lower for an easier version.

FOUNDATIONS

- Fetch (page 41)

MATERIALS

- Ball
- Hoop (toy basketball hoop, trash can)

STEPS

1. Use shaping to teach your dog to stick their nose into the hoop. Position the hoop between you and your dog. Reward any movement toward the hoop. Increase your criteria by rewarding only when your dog interacts with the hoop with their nose, until they figure out to dunk their nose inside. Reward with a treat inside the hoop, to help encourage the behavior.

2. Set the hoop aside and practice a few repetitions of cueing "Fetch" to your hand with the ball.

(continued)

Teach your dog to target the hoop with their nose.

PLAY BASKETBALL (CONTINUED)

3. Combine the skills from steps 1 and 2. With the hoop in front of you, ask your dog to fetch the ball. Reward if they bring it near the hoop, even if they don't place it inside yet. Repeat, jackpotting once they get it inside the hoop! If your dog needs support, place your hand over the hoop to help guide them initially.
4. Once your dog is consistently putting the ball in the hoop, add a verbal cue, such as "dunk it," before they fetch the ball.
5. To make this trick more impressive, stand farther away from the hoop so your dog learns to make a basket independently.

TIP: If you are having trouble shaping step 1, you could use luring or cue "Touch" (page 24) with your hand over the hoop, to teach your dog to target the hoop.

RIDE A SKATEBOARD

Forget the dog park; let's head to the skate park! In this trick, your dog will learn to ride a skateboard with three paws on the board and one paw pushing off the ground. Other variations of this trick include teaching your dog to hop onto the skateboard with all four paws so that it rolls forward, or teaching them to put just their front paws on the board. These versions are "easier" to teach, but can cause the board to roll too quickly on smooth surfaces.

When teaching this trick, take time to get your dog comfortable around the skateboard and acclimate them to its movement. Hold the skateboard tightly to prevent its moving out from under them too quickly at first. Smaller dogs can perform this trick using a regular skateboard, and larger dogs can use a longboard.

MATERIALS

- Skateboard

STEPS

1. Get your dog comfortable with the skateboard by moving it around near them and rewarding as it rolls and makes noise. Hold the board still and use shaping or luring to encourage your dog to put all four paws on it. Gently move the skateboard back and forth with them on it, rewarding throughout.

2. Lure or shape your dog to step onto the board with just three paws, one rear paw remaining on the ground. Practice until they consistently mount the skateboard with three paws. Keep the skateboard still throughout this process.

(continued)

RIDE A SKATEBOARD (CONTINUED)

3. With three paws on the board, slowly lure your dog to lean forward. Mark and reward when they step forward with the paw that's on the floor. Hold the skateboard so it doesn't shoot forward, but still allow your dog to push it a bit. Alternatively, slowly drag the skateboard forward yourself, rewarding when your dog steps their back paw as it moves, then transition to luring.
4. Progress until your dog can push the board multiple steps while you're still guiding the board. Slowly reduce how much you are holding the board until they can control it independently, staying ready to catch the board if needed.
5. Fade out the lure and add a verbal cue, such as "skateboard."

TIP: When teaching your dog to put three paws on the board, you can use a skill, such as "Pivot" (page 179), to help your dog sidestep one rear paw off the board, or place a small target on the ground to help them understand where that rear paw should be.

PLAY THE PIANO

Teach your dog to play the piano and become the next Beethoven! This trick is perfect for dogs who love to use their paws in such tricks as "Front Paws Up" (page 30), or "Wipe Your Paws" (page 98). For a fun twist, teach your dog to "Speak" (see page 49) and sing a song while they play their keyboard!

Toy pianos work great for this trick. Dogs of most sizes can put their paws up on a children's piano that is elevated off the ground; just be sure to stabilize the piano or position it against the wall if it tips over easily. Larger dogs (or small dogs sitting on a stool) could also learn to play a real piano, if you have one!

FOUNDATIONS

- Front Paws Up (page 30)

MATERIALS

- Toy piano

STEPS

1. Get your dog used to the sounds of the piano. Press the keys a few times, rewarding your dog as the sounds play.
2. Cue "Front Paws Up" on the piano. Mark and reward when your dog steps on the keys.
3. Lure your dog side to side to step on the keys and "play" the piano. If they know "Wipe Your Paws" (page 98), you could use their "dig" cue to encourage them to swipe at the piano keys.
4. Once your dog is stepping on the keys multiple times, fade out the lure. Move your hand from side to side without a treat, and wiggle your fingers, as if you're playing the piano, to introduce a hand signal. Practice until you can cue with just the hand signal.
5. Add a verbal cue, such as "play a song," before asking your dog to play!

TIP: If your dog is unsure about putting their front paws up, try cueing "Shake" (page 27) with your hand near the keys, to teach your dog to press them. You could also use a treat to lure them to touch the keys.

GET IN A SUITCASE

If your dog wistfully watches you pack your suitcase for every trip, this is the trick for them! In this trick, your dog will nudge open the lid of a suitcase and lie down inside. While teaching your dog to hop into an open suitcase is quite simple, teaching them to open the lid is what makes this trick extra impressive.

When teaching this trick, be sure to select a suitcase that is large enough to fit your dog when they're lying down. Lay a thick blanket in the bottom of the suitcase to cushion it, otherwise they will be lying on the hard handles.

⚠ **SAFETY FIRST:** Never zip your dog inside the suitcase or move the suitcase while your dog is inside. Store suitcases so your dog could not accidentally get inside them except during supervised training sessions.

FOUNDATIONS

- Down (page 23)

MATERIALS

- Suitcase
- Blanket

STEPS

1. With the suitcase completely open, use luring or shaping to teach your dog to get inside with all four paws. Reward while your dog is standing entirely in the suitcase, then toss a treat out of the suitcase to reset.

2. Cue your dog to lie down after they get into the suitcase and reward while they're lying down. Repeat the sequence of getting in the suitcase, then lying down, until your dog automatically lies down once they get into the suitcase.

(continued)

3

Hold the lid partly closed and cue your dog to get in.

GET IN A SUITCASE (CONTINUED)

3. Hold the suitcase lid partially closed and cue your dog to get in. Repeat, gradually holding the suitcase more closed every few repetitions. Eventually, your dog will need to wedge their nose between the suitcase and the lid to fit through. Jackpot when they do! Continue until your dog can get in the suitcase with the lid almost entirely closed.

4. Rest the suitcase lid closed, offset slightly to leave a small lip where your dog can nudge the suitcase, and cue your dog to get in. Reward if they try to nudge their way in, even if not successful at first, until they can successfully push open the lid and get into the suitcase on their own.

5. Add a verbal cue, such as "pack up," before asking your dog to get in the suitcase.

TIP: Drape a towel or cut pool noodle over one edge of the suitcase to leave a larger gap if your dog needs help nudging the lid open.

PICK A CARD

Get your dog ready to put on a magic show or play a game of Go Fish by teaching them how to pick a card! For their next trick, your dog will pull one card out of a few held in your hand. For dogs who already know the trick "Hold" (page 37), this trick is a simple extension. Some dogs may be unsure about the feeling of paper in their mouth, so they'll need some time to get used to holding a card without spitting it back out. Use a deck of cards that you're not attached to, as they will likely end up covered in slobber and teeth marks!

FOUNDATIONS

- Hold (page 37)

MATERIALS

- Deck of cards

STEPS

1. Hold a single playing card in front of your dog and cue "Hold." Practice several times so they get used to taking the card out of your hand.
2. Teach your dog to pull the card out of your hand. You can do this by cueing "Tug" (page 38), asking your dog to back up a step (page 60), or even just saying your dog's name so that they look up at you, pulling the card as they do. Some dogs may naturally pull the card out of your hand when you cue "Hold;" if so, you are already ready for step 3!
3. Hold a few cards spaced out in your hand. Cue your dog to take a card and reward when they pull one out.
4. Add a verbal cue, such as "pick a card," before asking your dog to grab the card.

DOWN

READ CUE CARDS

This trick will leave everyone wondering, "How did they do that??" The secret is quite simple! In this sleight of hand, your dog will "read" words on a stack of notecards and perform the tricks written on them, without you saying anything. While it looks as if your dog is recognizing the word on the card, they are actually responding to the position you're holding the card in!

This trick uses a cue transfer to create a new visual cue for a trick your dog already knows. For example, you could teach them that when you hold the card at your chest, they should sit. The key to making this trick convincing is choosing ways to position the cards that are subtle enough that your audience won't catch on, but distinct enough that your dog can tell the difference.

MATERIALS

- Notecards

STEPS

1. Choose a trick your dog knows well on a verbal cue (e.g., "Down," page 23) and add the "secret cue" (e.g., holding the card at waist level). Move the card into the position in an overly exaggerated way, then cue the trick (e.g., move the card down to your waist, then say "down"). Mark and reward when your dog does the trick. Repeat many times.

2. Move the card into position and pause before saying your cue. If your dog does the trick without your saying their normal cue, jackpot! Continue practicing, using your verbal cue as needed, until your dog will consistently perform the trick with only the notecard position as a cue.

3. Gradually make the visual notecard cue more subtle until the movement is almost unnoticeable, as if you are just naturally showing your dog the card.

4. Repeat steps 1–3 to teach your dog a distinctive "secret cue" for a different trick. (Ideas: at chest height for "sit," in one hand to the right or left for "spin," or out toward your dog for "back up.")

5. Teach your dog to distinguish between the cues by practicing one cue, then the other. You may have to use your verbal cues to help them remember the difference at first. Practice cueing the tricks in different orders, sometimes cueing the same trick twice in a row, until they are consistently able to "read" the words correctly. Repeat steps 1–5 for each new "word" you want to introduce!

BRAIN BREAK

PAW-CASSO PAINTING

Teaching your dog to paint with a brush (see page 123) is an impressive way to give your dog the chance to be an artist, but for a simpler project, try this painting enrichment activity! To create their artwork, all your dog has to do is lick some food off a plastic bag that has a paint-covered canvas inside. Licking can have a calming effect for dogs, so this activity is a great way to help them chill out while making a unique piece of art in the process!

MATERIALS

- Canvas or paper
- Nontoxic, washable paint
- Spreadable treat (e.g., peanut butter, yogurt, applesauce)
- Plastic storage bag
- Painter's tape

STEPS

1. Space apart drops of nontoxic, washable paint all over your canvas.
2. Spread a thin layer of peanut butter or another dog-safe food on the outside of one side of the plastic storage bag.
3. Carefully slide the canvas into the bag, paint and treat side up, and seal it tightly.
4. Tape the bag to the floor to keep it in place (or place it in the grass outside).
5. Allow your dog to lick off the topping; they will spread the paint inside around with their tongue as they do so!
6. Carefully remove the canvas from the bag and allow it to dry.
7. Hang your dog's artwork on the wall for all to enjoy!

Supplies

2

Dollop paint on canvas and spread food on bag.

3

Seal canvas inside bag.

7

Enjoy your dog's artwork!

THE CIRCUS DOG

It's time for your dog to take center stage for the performance of a lifetime! Even if your dog's version of the "big top" is just your living room, these tricks are the perfect stunts to turn them into a star. The tricks in this section involve dancing, jumping, and impressive acrobatics that are sure to wow any audience. Grab your top hat and let's get started

⚠ **SAFETY FIRST:** Many of the tricks in this section require a great deal of athleticism from your dog and should only be attempted with dogs who are physically sound. Tricks marked with the ⚠ icon are not safe for puppies whose growth plates have not closed, or for dogs with physical limitations, such as dogs with joint or back issues.

JUMP THROUGH A HOOP

Every circus dog needs to learn to jump through a hoop! This trick is great for building confidence around strange objects. For an added challenge, cover the hoop with loose streamers or a sheet of tissue paper for them to burst through! For puppies who are too young to jump, you can practice a safe version of this trick where your dog simply walks through the hoop at ground level, without jumping.

Most hula hoops are filled with beads that make noise when it moves. If your dog is sensitive to noises, you can purchase detachable hula hoops that are not filled. To make a larger hoop, duct tape two pool noodles together to form a circle; for a smaller hoop, try a floral or embroidery hoop from a craft store.

⚠ Not safe for puppies or dogs with joint/back issues

MATERIALS

- Hoop

STEPS

1. Get your dog comfortable around the hoop by gently moving it around so it makes noise, rewarding your dog throughout. Lay the hoop on the ground and reward any interaction with the hoop. Encourage your dog to walk over it and try cueing them to do simple tricks (e.g., "Sit," "Spin," "Shake") while standing inside the hoop.
2. Hold the hoop upright between you and a wall, with the bottom edge resting on the ground. With your dog waiting on one side of the hoop, toss a treat to the other side. Mark as your dog goes through the hoop to get the treat. Repeat, going both directions.
3. Gesture sideways without actually tossing a treat, rewarding once your dog goes through. Practice until you can cue them through with a subtle gesture.
4. Gradually increase the height at which you hold the hoop so your dog has to jump through it. (Keep the hoop on the ground for puppies and other dogs who shouldn't jump.) Move the hoop away from the wall.
5. Add a verbal cue, such as "jump," "through," or "hoop," before your dog jumps through.

JUMP THROUGH HOOPED ARMS

While "Jump Through a Hoop" (page 148) is a great circus trick, an even more impressive variation is to use your arms as the hoop! Cueing your dog to jump through your arms from each direction creates a very dynamic and exciting performance.

Position the arm opposite your dog as the bottom of your hooped arms, for the smoothest jumps. Small dogs will have likely no problem fitting through your arms, and many larger dogs may surprise you by streamlining their body to glide through your arms. To make the hoop larger, hold a rope or disk between your hands. Practice on a padded, nonslip surface, limit repetitions, and hold your arms at an appropriate height, to keep your dog safe.

⚠ Not safe for puppies or dogs with joint/back issues

STEPS

1. Sit facing a wall, with your dog at your left side. Place a treat across from them, giving them enough space to jump and land. Stretch out your right arm toward the wall, low to the ground, and release your dog to get the treat, marking when they go over your arm. Repeat, switching arms to practice both directions.

2. Gradually raise the height of your arm, so your dog has to jump over it.

3. Repeat steps 1 and 2, adding the other arm to create a large hoop shape against the wall for your dog to jump through. Begin adding a verbal cue, such as "through" or "hoop."

4. Cue your dog through your arms without placing a treat across from them, jackpotting when they go through.

Teach your dog to jump over one arm.

5. Gradually move away from the wall, cueing your dog to jump through your hooped arms in each direction. Progress until they will jump through your arms, completely away from the wall!

BOING

Teach your dog to jump for joy! In this trick, they will jump straight up in the air with all four paws. "Boing" serves as the foundation for other impressive tricks, such as jumping rope, and is a great way to show off your dog's excitement on its own. Teaching "Boing" by building off "Touch" (page 24) is a great way to teach the trick in a controlled manner. You could instead hold a tempting treat or toy above your dog, to encourage them to jump up.

Since this is a high-impact trick, it's not a good fit for puppies or older dogs who need to limit jumping. For all dogs, train on a padded, nonslip surface, and practice in short sessions to avoid overexerting your dog.

⚠ Not safe for puppies or dogs with joint/back issues

FOUNDATIONS

- Touch (page 24)

STEPS

1. Practice a few normal repetitions of cueing "Touch." Gradually raise your hand higher, above your dog's head, until they have to look up to touch your hand.
2. Continue to increase the height until your dog hops off the ground with their front paws to touch your hand. Jackpot when they lift their front paws.
3. Progress until your dog has to jump with all four paws to reach your hand. Jackpot when they jump off the ground.
4. Once your dog is jumping consistently, begin fading out the "Touch" cue and simply raise your hand up above their head. Reward when they jump in response to the hand signal.
5. Add a new verbal cue, such as "Boing" or "Hop," before using your hand signal to cue your dog to jump.

FOOTSIES

This trick takes the adorable picture of a young child dancing with their feet on their parent's toes and gives it a canine twist! "Footsies" is a great trick for performances and for photos. Try taking steps forward or backward together, or kick your feet back and forth in a cancan-style dance move.

To keep this trick distinct from your "Peekaboo" (page 73) cue, you could teach your dog to go behind you from one side for the cue "Peekaboo" and from the other side for the cue "Footsies." Alternatively, you can add a different visual cue, such as wiggling your feet, to cue your dog to do "Footsies" rather than just stopping in the center position.

FOUNDATIONS

- Peekaboo (page 73)

STEPS

1. Practice a few normal repetitions of cueing "Peekaboo." Then, turn your toes inward and cue "Peekaboo." Lure as needed to encourage your dog to step onto your feet. Mark and reward even if they just put one paw on your foot. Progress until your dog will put both paws on your feet automatically.

2. Move your feet farther apart every few repetitions, until your dog can place their paws on your feet around shoulder-width apart.

(continued)

Turn your toes inward and lure or cue "Peekaboo."

FOOTSIES (CONTINUED)

3. Introduce movement: Pick up one foot and reward your dog for keeping their paws on your feet. Practice until you can move each foot a few times with your dog remaining in position.
4. Take one small step forward, then add more steps as your dog is successful. Lure, if needed, to encourage them to move forward. Continue until you can take multiple steps together without luring.
5. Add a verbal cue like "footsies" to cue your dog to come into position and perform this trick!

Try starting with your shoes between your feet.

TIP: If your dog is struggling, try teaching them to put their front paws on a pair of shoes first. Then, place the shoes between your feet and cue your dog to come into the middle position, luring as needed to help them place their paws on the shoes. Finally, put the shoes on!

CHORUS LINE KICKS

Prepare your dog for the big stage by teaching them their own version of chorus line kicks! Rather than being a never-ending line of dancers, the canine version of this move involves just you and your pup. Your dog will stand between your feet and wave each paw as you kick your feet, creating an in-sync dance move.

Before learning this trick, your dog will need to know how to "Wave" (page 68) with each paw. Instead of doing this trick in a middle position, you could try it instead with them standing at your side. For a different variation that's slightly easier, have your dog sit facing you and cue them to lift each paw as your lift your feet, to create a mirror image!

FOUNDATIONS

- Shake (page 27)
- Peekaboo (page 73)
- Wave (page 68)

STEPS

1. Practice a few normal repetitions of cueing "Shake" with each paw. Then, cue your dog to come into a "Peekaboo" position. Reach down and cue "Shake" with your right hand for the right paw, then with your left hand for the left paw, marking and rewarding for each.

(continued)

Cue "Shake" with your dog standing between your feet.

CHORUS LINE KICKS (CONTINUED)

2. Reach down and cue "Wave" with each paw as you did with "Shake" in step 1. Practice until your dog can switch fluently between waving each paw.
3. Use a cue transfer to teach your dog to lift each paw as you lift the corresponding foot. Kick your right foot forward, then cue "Wave" with the right paw. Repeat until your dog lifts their paw when you just raise your foot.
4. Repeat step 3 with the other paw.
5. Practice kicking with one foot, then the other, repeating to create the back and forth "Chorus Line Kicks" pattern. Your dog may temporarily need you to support with hand signals again until they get the sequence down!

AROUND A CONE

Teaching your dog to go around a cone is an entertaining circus trick that is simple for many dogs to learn. Wrapping around a cone in each direction is a great way to help your dog stretch and bend, and it can also help build skills for such tricks as "Figure 8" (page 163) and "Airplane Arms" (page 165). Try shaking up this trick by asking your dog to go around a variety of different props, or take this trick on the road by asking them to wrap around trees, posts, and other objects in the wild!

MATERIALS

- Cone (or similarly shaped object)

STEPS

1. With your dog at your right side, use your right hand to lure them counterclockwise around the cone in a U shape. Mark once they turn around the back side of the cone and toss the treat ahead of your dog to encourage them to drive forward.
2. Fade out the lure by repeating the motion from step 1 without a treat in hand; reward by tossing a treat with the opposite hand. Progress until you can cue your dog around the cone by just sweeping your hand toward it.
3. Gradually send your dog around the cone from farther away.
4. Add a verbal cue, such as "around" or "wrap," before cueing your dog around the cone.
5. Repeat steps 1–4 using your left hand, starting with your dog on your left side, to teach your dog to wrap the other way. Use distinctive body language and/or a new verbal cue to tell your dog which direction you want them to go.

FIGURE 8

Teaching your dog to weave through your legs in a figure 8 motion is a flashy trick to showcase your dog's flexibility and athleticism! The end goal of this trick is for you to remain mostly still as your dog wraps around your legs in a figure 8 shape. If needed, you can lean from side to side, to help provide a visual cue for your dog to perform this trick.

Although this trick may be more challenging for taller dogs, large dogs can often still learn to do it by ducking under you and making wider turns. You may have to lean more from side to side or even scissor-step forward and backward to give them enough room to weave through. Once you master "Figure 8," give "Leg Weaves" (page 169) a try, for a twist on this trick!

STEPS

1. Stand with your feet apart and your dog at your left side. Hold a treat in each hand. Reach behind your right leg with your right hand, to lure your dog to weave in front of your left leg and behind your right, ending and rewarding at your right side. Repeat in the other direction (reach behind your left leg with your left hand, etc.). Lean in the direction your dog is moving in as you lure, to help when fading out the lure later.

2. Once your dog can follow the lures smoothly for the full figure 8, hold a treat only in the second hand. Lure with an empty hand for the first half of the 8, then with the treat for the second half.

(continued)

Lure your dog to weave in a figure 8 pattern.

FIGURE 8 (CONTINUED)

3. Reduce the lure to simply pointing with your hand (no treat lure) as you lean to each side to cue your dog through your legs. Lean, then point, as your dog continues to learn the figure 8 pattern more fluently.
4. Try simply leaning from side to side without using your hands as a cue. Jackpot if your dog weaves through your legs!
5. Add a verbal cue, such as "eight," before you begin leaning. Over time, you can make the leaning more subtle as your dog weaves through your legs independently.

NOTE: You can switch the direction of this trick to start on the right side, if you prefer; just switch the directions noted in these steps.

JUMP OVER AIRPLANE ARMS

Similar to "Jump Through Hooped Arms" (page 151), in this trick, your dog will use your arms as jumps! This is a fast-paced trick involving you holding your arms outstretched like airplane wings as your dog circles around you, jumping over each arm as they go.

For your dog to perform this trick smoothly, they first need to learn to go around you in a circle on the ground. Building this pattern before introducing the jumping component will help your dog perform this trick as a more fluid motion. While it's not necessarily a prerequisite, dogs who are familiar with "Jump Through Hooped Arms" will have an advantage toward learning the jumping portion of this trick. If your dog struggles with the jumping piece, try starting with that trick!

⚠ Not safe for puppies or dogs with joint/back issues

STEPS

1. Sit on the floor with your dog in front of you and a treat in each hand. Lure your dog to circle halfway around you, rewarding once they are behind you, then continue the lure with the other hand to complete a full circle.

2. Fade out the lure by cueing your dog to go behind you with an empty hand, then lure just for the second half of the circle. Practice until your dog will circle all the way around you without a lure. Try sequencing multiple circles together.

(continued)

Teach your dog to circle around you on the ground.

JUMP OVER AIRPLANE ARMS (CONTINUED)

3. Sit in a hallway or between a wall and a tall object, such as a chair. Hold one arm horizontally toward the wall that your dog passes in the second half of the circle. Cue them to go around you; after they go behind you, they will need to jump over your arm. Use a treat, if needed, to encourage them to do the jump. Repeat until your dog can fluently circle around you and jump over one arm.

4. Extend both arms horizontally and cue your dog to circle you. If needed, you can place a treat behind you at first, to encourage them to jump the first arm. Give your dog extra cues and support as needed, until they can circle around you, jumping over both arms.

5. Gradually move away from the walls until your dog can jump circles around you without barriers. Add a verbal cue, such as "airplane," to cue them to jump over your arms.

LEG WEAVES

You may have seen dogs on an agility course speeding back and forth through weave poles. In this trick, your dog will instead weave back and forth through your legs as you walk forward! This trick is very similar to "Figure 8" (page 163), but introduces the element of moving forward. This version can actually be easier for many dogs, as the steps forward become a clear visual cue and give your dog more room to navigate.

STEPS

1. Start with your dog at your left side and a treat in each hand. Step forward with your right leg, then reach your right hand behind it to lure your dog through; mark and reward. Repeat with the opposite side, stepping forward with your left leg and luring your dog through with your left hand.
2. Once you can sequence four or more lured steps in a row, hold treats only in your left hand and reward every other step (lure with an empty hand to the right, lure with a treat in hand to the left and reward, repeat). Then, try reducing your rewards to every three or four steps.
3. Fade the lure to a subtler point to cue your dog to weave through your legs. Step, then point, repeating for several steps. Reward more often at first, to help reinforce your dog for following the subtler cues.
4. Try stepping forward and not giving any hand signals. Jackpot if your dog weaves through!
5. Add a verbal cue, such as "weave" or "through," before you step.

Step forward and lure your dog through your legs.

NOTE: You can switch the direction of this trick to start at your right side, if you prefer; just switch the directions noted in these steps.

HANDSTAND

Every circus acrobat needs to learn a handstand! In this variation, your dog will learn to do a handstand with their front paws on the ground and their rear paws on a slanted platform or wall. This trick requires a great deal of athleticism from your dog, so only attempt with physically fit dogs. Practice in short sessions, and only progress as far as your dog is comfortable. The final trick doesn't need to be a completely vertical handstand; you can stop at whatever incline you and your dog are comfortable with.

Use a sturdy platform with a textured surface, such as a yoga mat or traction tape, to prevent slipping. Be sure your platform is always secure as you increase the incline, so it doesn't tip over!

⚠ Not safe for puppies or dogs with joint/back issues

FOUNDATIONS

- Rear Foot Target (page 33)

MATERIALS

- Platform

STEPS

1. Practice cueing your dog to back up to a rear foot target. After several repetitions, raise the platform to a slight incline. Repeat, continuing to increase the angle slightly, every few successful repetitions.

2. Eventually, your dog will have to lift their rear end into a more vertical position to balance on the target. Keep these repetitions short at first and spaced out over many training sessions as your dog learns to balance.

3. Practice until your dog can back up to a nearly vertical platform, either walking their feet up the platform or lifting them up behind them to go into a handstand position.

Practice backing onto an angled platform.

4. **OPTIONAL:** To transition this behavior to a wall, first hang a yoga mat or another material with traction against the wall. Practice several repetitions with the platform leaning against the wall, then remove the platform and cue again. Reward any effort toward your dog placing their back paws on the wall until they can lift them up into a handstand position.

5. Add a verbal cue, such as "handstand," before cueing your trick!

DOG CATCH

It's the perfect end to a performance: your dog leaps into your arms for a huge celebration! "Dog Catch" is a trick that involves a lot of trust from both parties. To perform this trick safely, it's important to teach it correctly so that you and your dog are prepared to work as a team.

This trick is not a safe choice for puppies, since it involves jumping, but you can build the foundations by practicing at ground level, without jumping, when your dog is young. When teaching this trick for very small dogs, sit on a low step stool or even just kneel on the ground for steps 1 and 2, then crouch down as much as needed for the final trick. This trick requires strength and coordination on the handler's part, and there is an upward size limit for dogs; you know your limits best!

⚠ Not safe for puppies or dogs with joint/back issues

MATERIALS

- Chair
- Pillows

STEPS

1. Teach your dog to jump into your lap from the side while you're sitting. For some dogs, you can simply pat your legs. For others, you may need to sit on the floor and use a treat to lure them onto your lap, then gradually transition to a chair. You can put a blanket, pillow, or cushion on your lap, to provide some padding and an easier target for your dog, if needed.
2. Once your dog will consistently jump into your lap, gradually increase the angle to be closer to standing/vertical by adding one pillow at a time underneath you. As you practice, wrap your arms around your dog as if catching them. Monitor your dog's comfort as you do this; it's important that they are comfortable with handling before proceeding with this trick, to ensure they enjoy it, too!

(continued)

DOG CATCH (CONTINUED)

3. When your dog can jump into your lap when you are almost standing, practice the same progression as step 2 by doing a wall sit rather than sitting on a chair. Slowly increase the height until your dog can jump into your arms when you are leaning against the wall, close to fully upright.

4. Take a step away from the wall and cue your dog to jump into your arms. Squat as much as needed to help them be successful. Move farther away from the wall as you continue to practice.

5. Add a verbal cue, such as "catch," to cue this trick.

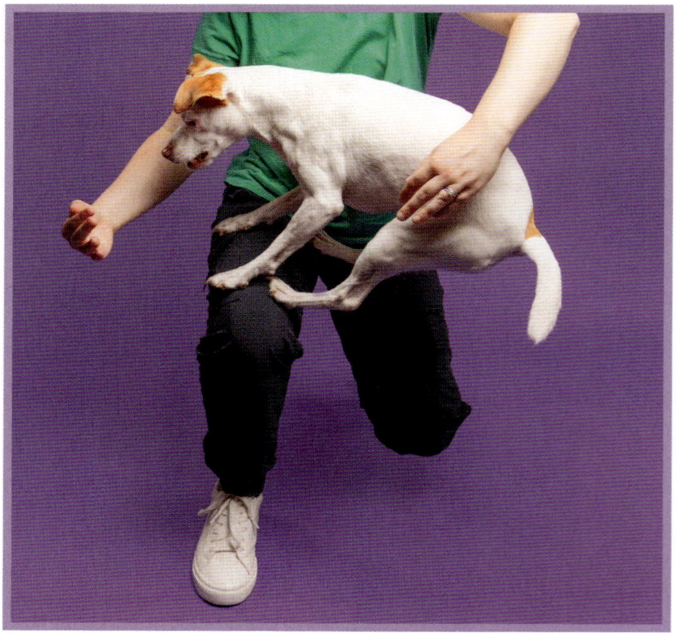

Crouch down to make this trick more accessible for small dogs.

REBOUND

"Rebound" is an impressive stunt in which your dog bounces off your legs with all four paws, turning in an arc to land back on the ground. When teaching this trick, many of the steps overlap with the process for teaching "Dog Catch" (page 173), but your dog doesn't have to know it before learning "Rebound."

This trick requires a lot physically from your dog, so be sure to only teach this trick if they are physically capable. Practice on a padded, nonslip surface so they can land safely, and limit the number of repetitions to avoid overexerting your dog. Teach this skill over many training sessions, to give your dog time to build up the flexibility and muscle memory needed to be successful.

⚠ Not safe for puppies or dogs with joint/back issues

MATERIALS

- Chair
- Pillows

STEPS

1. Envision the space around you as a clock face parallel to the floor, with 12 o'clock in front of you. Sit in a chair and position your dog at about 10 o'clock, then call them into your lap. Mark once they land in your lap, then promptly toss a treat to the opposite side (around the 2 o'clock position) to reward. This will begin to pattern the rebound motion.

2. Slowly transition to a standing position by adding one pillow at a time underneath you. As you move higher, your dog will eventually not be able to fully land in your lap before jumping off to retrieve the treat; they will have to "rebound" off your legs in one fluid motion.

(continued)

Sit on pillows so your dog begins to jump off your legs at an angle

REBOUND (CONTINUED)

3. Fade out the treat by patting your lap to cue your dog up, then flicking your hand as if tossing a treat. Reward from your treat pouch once they successfully land on the ground.
4. Transition to doing a wall sit, repeating the motion from steps 2 and 3 and gradually working toward a standing position.
5. Take a step away from the wall and cue your dog to rebound. Continue to practice until you can cue this trick completely away from the wall. Add a verbal cue, such as "rebound," before cueing your dog to jump!

NOTE: You can teach this trick in either direction. After your dog learns "Rebound" in one direction, you can restart the process and teach them to flip the opposite way!

TIP: If you need help getting your dog to jump into your lap, read step 1 of "Dog Catch" (page 173).

PIVOT

Pivoting around a target is not only a great circus trick, but also a very beneficial dog-training exercise! In this trick, your dog will keep their front paws on a target while stepping their back paws around in a circle. Dogs naturally operate in "front-wheel drive" and need to learn how to use their back paws independently, and this trick is an excellent way to do so! This is helpful for teaching such tricks as "Orbit" (page 180) and can improve your dog's overall coordination.

FOUNDATIONS

- Front Paws Up (page 30)

MATERIALS

- Foot target

STEPS

1. Cue your dog to put their front paws up on a target, facing you. Reward them several times for just keeping their front paws on the target. Toss a treat away to reset your dog, then move to a different position relative to the target and cue "Front Paws Up" again.

2. With your dog's front paws on the target, take a few small steps to one side, and mark and reward as soon as they step with their back paws to mirror you. Repeat, switching directions occasionally, until your dog will pivot one or more steps with their back paws to mirror your movement.

3. Gradually increase the number of steps your dog takes before you reward until they can pivot a full circle around. Add a hand signal, such as holding your hand straight in front of you and/or a verbal cue, such as "pivot" or "step."

4. **OPTIONAL:** Teach your dog to pivot without your stepping around with them. Give your hand and/or verbal cue and take more subtle steps, rewarding them for pivoting any steps without your rotating. Gradually reduce how much you step, and work up to relying more on your hand/verbal cues until your dog can pivot with those cues alone.

TIP: If your dog doesn't step sideways to mirror you, try luring their head toward one shoulder, marking and rewarding when they step their back paws in the opposite direction.

ORBIT

"Orbit" is a challenging and stunning trick in which your dog circles backward around you in a fluid motion. To learn this trick, your dog needs to have very strong rear-end awareness built through such skills as "Pivot" (page 179). Although teaching "Rear Foot Target" (page 33) isn't required for this trick, it's another great way to practice rear-end awareness to get your dog ready. Teaching "Orbit" slowly, over many sessions, is the best way to help them develop the muscle memory to perform it smoothly.

When teaching this trick, you'll need one or two foot targets. To help your dog learn to keep their body close to you as they wrap around, it can also be helpful to build a box around you to help guide their body and prevent them from swinging out too widely. You can stand with the corner of a wall or couch behind you and close off the remainder of the square using such items as chairs, ottomans, X pens, or anything else you have on hand.

FOUNDATIONS

- Pivot (page 179)

MATERIALS

- 1-2 foot targets
- Items to create barriers (see intro)

STEPS

1. Practice a few repetitions of "Pivot;" your dog should be able to pivot around without you walking with them. Position yourself inside a box, as described in the introduction. Place a target at your left side and cue "Front Paws Up" (page 30) with your dog facing forward. Cue them to pivot so that their rear end is rotating counterclockwise. Continue this pivot motion until their rear end is wrapping behind you and your body is in the way of their pivoting any further.

(continued)

Cue or lure your dog to pivot behind you.

ORBIT (CONTINUED)

2. Repeat step 1 to teach the other half of the orbit, instead placing a target at your right side and beginning with your dog facing backward. They should still be pivoting in the same direction (counterclockwise), to wrap their rear end in front of you.

3. Combine steps 1 and 2 so your dog rotates in a full circle around you. If you have two targets, place one at each side and cue your dog to rotate the back half until their front paws are on the second target, reward, then cue them to rotate the front half. If you have only one target, place it at your left side, rewarding halfway as you guide your dog to pivot all the way around. Use a food lure to support this process, as needed. Continue to sequence these steps together until your dog can smoothly rotate a full circle around you without luring, rewarding only at the end.

4. Remove the supports. Take away the foot target(s) and practice orbiting a full circle. Then, remove the sides of your "box" until your dog can orbit with no barrier around you.

5. Add a verbal cue, such as "orbit," before cueing your dog to back around you.

Cue or lure your dog to pivot in front of you.

NOTE: You can switch the direction of this trick to start at your right side and rotate clockwise, if you prefer; just switch the directions noted in these steps. After your dog learns to orbit one way, you can repeat the process to teach the other direction!

BRAIN BREAK

OLD TOYS, NEW GAMES

Playing with your dog is a great way to give them an outlet for natural canine behaviors. Your dog may be genetically wired for retrieving and enjoy fetching a ball, or they may have a strong prey drive and want nothing more than to tear apart a squeaky toy. The type of play each dog enjoys depends on factors such as their breed or mix, individual preferences, and past experiences. The next time you are wrapping up a training session or looking to help your dog get some mental and physical exercise, try one of these games to shake up the way you play!

- **Hide-and-Seek:** Activate your dog's seeking system by hiding a toy for them to find. Start by concealing a toy in an easy spot as your dog watches. Then, have your dog wait out of sight until you release them to find the toy. Progressively hide the toy in more challenging spots as your dog catches on to the game. When your dog finds the toy, reward them with their favorite kind of play! This is a great low-impact alternative to throwing a toy for your dog to retrieve over and over again, and adds an extra level of mental stimulation as your dog searches to find their beloved toy.

- **Blanket Burrow:** For dogs who love to dig, try hiding their favorite toy under a blanket. Start by only partially covering the toy, then gradually bury it deeper into the blanket. Reward your dog with play once they get the toy out! Squeaky toys work great for this game, since you can squeak them to entice your dog to dig them out. Try burying a few toys at one time, if your dog enjoys this activity!

- **Ready, Set, Go:** Before throwing a toy or engaging in a game of tug, slowly drag the toy along the ground so that your dog watches or "stalks" it. After they calmly watch the toy for a moment, excitedly engage in play! As your dog catches on to the routine, you can increase how long you let them "stalk" the toy before you toss or tug with it. Say "ready, set" as you drag the toy, then say "go!" once it's time for them to get the toy!

In loving memory of Rigby and Brisket

ACKNOWLEDGMENTS

So many people (and pets) played an integral part in bringing this book to life. "Thank you" isn't enough to express my gratitude toward . . .

. . . Luna, for inspiring my love of trick training, being the most eager and forgiving learning partner, and keeping me company throughout the writing process.

. . . my husband, Caleb, for encouraging me to pursue every dream and having full confidence in me even when I have none.

. . . the entire team at Page Street Publishing, for working to make this book a reality. Special thanks to: Marissa Giambelluca, my editor, for seeing the potential in this project and patiently seeing it through to the end; and to Elena Van Horn, my designer, for her creative direction in turning this book into a visual masterpiece.

. . . Holly Hildreth, for her brilliant photography work in capturing dozens of *trick-y* action shots and poses. Her stunning photos truly make the tricks jump off the page!

. . . the talented dogs who expertly demonstrated every trick, and their fabulous owners.

. . . and every single social media follower, for supporting our journey in sharing the joy of trick training with people around the world. Without you, I never would have had the opportunity to write this book. From the bottom of my heart, thank you!

MEET THE MODELS

LUNA is a seven-year-old mixed breed (mostly Chihuahua and American pit bull terrier!), owned by author Kaylin Haugen. She believes cheese and chasing small critters are the greatest joys in life. Luna loves learning tricks and training in such sports as barn hunt and agility, but her favorite pastime is popping people's personal bubbles to snuggle with them or lick their faces.

GARY, a seven-year-old mixed breed, and his owner, Sarah Johnson, met at a bereavement program for grieving families and health care workers. He loves people, being outside, and training for scent work, rally, and obedience. Gary recently passed his test to become a therapy dog!

CAPRICORN, owned by Niki Hird, VMD, is a five-year-old German shepherd who excels in agility, scent work, and rally; she's a therapy dog, too! Capricorn is incredibly sweet and mellow, loves tennis balls, and despises floor lamps and sneezes.

CHESTER, a seven-year-old Labrador retriever, was born to be a service dog, but was adopted by his puppy raiser, Sophie Fitzhugh, after being released from the program. Now, he is an agility superstar and avid swimmer who is known for carrying around his prized possessions to show anyone who will look.

TRIP is a six-year-old Catahoula leopard dog who taught his owner, Michelle Lytle, to enjoy the unexpected. Although he isn't the high-drive dog she anticipated, he has excelled at learning tricks and trying his paw at other dog sports. He's clever, quirky, and enjoys being rewarded for his work with Arby's® or ice cream.

In Loving Memory of Rigby and Brisket

Just months after shooting this book, photographer Holly Hildreth heartbreakingly lost both of her beloved Pembroke Welsh corgis within a few weeks of each other. Rigby and Brisket were an inseparable pair and are deeply missed by all who had the honor of loving them.

RIGBY had a talent for filling every room he entered with love and light. In his 10 years, he was a star in front of the camera, and his smile graces the pages of calendars, greeting cards, and more. He never let being blind and diabetic slow him down and lived a life full of joy and adventure.

BRISKET brought laughter to every moment of his 4 years with his energetic and entertaining personality. He loved basking in the sun and barking at the people and chipmunks who dared to travel by his home. Brisket will always be remembered for spreading joy to everyone around him.

ABOUT THE AUTHOR

KAYLIN HAUGEN is, above all, an animal-lover. For as long as she can remember, she has loved learning about and caring for creatures big and small, from horses to hamsters, and has always found comfort and joy in the presence of a dog. She adopted her first dog of her own, a small mixed-breed named Luna, in April 2020. Together, they have mastered over 200 tricks and participated in a variety of competitive dog sports.

With a passion for using humane, rewards-based training methods, Kaylin is a Certified Trick Dog Instructor (CTDI) and teaches local trick training classes. She spreads the joy of dog tricks worldwide by sharing training tips via social media (@lunathetrickdog on Instagram). Kaylin is also a middle school teacher and lives in Columbus, Ohio, with her husband, Caleb, and their beloved Luna.

INDEX

O

P

R

S

T

U

V

W

Y